Faith
after the
Holocaust

❧

Eliezer Berkovits

KTAV PUBLISHING HOUSE, INC.

NEW YORK

1973

TABLE OF CONTENTS

FOREWORD

The main thesis of this volume was worked out during the critical weeks that led up to the Six Day War between Israel and the Arab nations, and was completed during those drama-filled six days; the last word of its heart was written practically when the last shot was fired in that war. It was written under almost unbearable tension, and against darkest fears and anxieties. The threat of another holocaust was hanging over Jewish people. This destruction would have been final for all Israel the world over, and not only for the Jewish people in the state of Israel. Our generation could not have survived another holocaust and, certainly, not this one. The state of Israel was a Jew's only comfort—although not really quite a healing one—after the extermination of six million of his people.

In spite of the fears and notwithstanding the tension, carried along by one's faith in the immortality of Judaism and the Jewish people, it was possible to write. That faith had to be affirmed anew with every word, for it was being tried and tested in the crucible of a fiery hour of Jewish and world destiny. Not once did I have to ask myself whether this faith in the eternity of Jewish survival was, perhaps, only a latter-day version of the "lying words," so radically rejected by the prophet Jeremiah: "The temple of the Lord, the temple of the Lord, the temple of the Lord." No, the State of Israel is not the temple of the Lord. But God can do without his temple; he cannot do without Israel, the people, nor can he, in this post-holocaust phase of world history, do without Israel, the state. It was this faith that I was affirming with every word I wrote in those critical weeks before the war and during the six days of the war. To wait and to see what was going to happen and then to write, would have been a betrayal and a desecration.

Since those days, the main thesis, which was meant to be essentially a confrontation with the holocaust of European Jewry, evolved into an examination of the Jewish experience in a holocaust world and of a world history of the holocaust spirit.

"A Theology of Intolerance," in Chapter 1, was published several years ago in the magazine, *Continuum;* the two sections of the second chapter, "Judaism in the Post-Christian Era" and the "Death of a God," in a somewhat different form, were previously published in *Judaism;* and part of "The Nemesis of Power History" in Chapter 5 also appeared previously in *Tradition.* They have been incorporated in this volume with the kind permission of these publications, to whom we hereby extend our thanks.

Eliezer Berkovits
22 Tammuz 5732
3 July 1972

INTRODUCTION

Approaching the Holocaust

There are two principle approaches to the holocaust of European Jewry: the attitude of pious submission to it as a manifestation of the divine will, and the more frequently met attitude of questioning and doubt, a position that may ultimately lead to outright rebellion against the very idea of a beneficent providence. The rebellion may reach quite deep, in which case it may appear as the Jewish version of contemporary radical theology. Its final emphasis may lie in the phrases that God is dead, and life, absurd. In truth, however, the decisive question is rather: Who is the one who truly relates to this awesome issue? is it not the person who actually experienced it himself, in his own body and soul? who actually entered the hell of the ghettos, the concentration camps, and the crematoria, with his wife and children, his family and friends, with innumerable fellow Jews from all over Europe, who lived, suffered, and endured, or who perished there? Or is it someone who read about it, heard about it, may have, perhaps, even experienced it in his identifying imagination? The response of these two cannot—dare not—be the same. Those who were there responded on the basis of their own experience, which was unique, incomparable, that stands in all human history in a class by itself. However much, and however deeply, those who were not there may identify with the sufferings of the victims, their experience remains forever, merely a vicarious shadow of the actual event, as removed from the reality of the holocaust as is the rather comfortable scholarship of the radical theologians of our day from the universe of the concentration camps and the crematoria. Their response, based on their vicarious experience, will be as shadowy and unreal as the experience itself. Needless to say, what applies to the rebellion of the

3

radical theologian applies with equal validity to the pious submission and the acceptance of the holocaust as an act of faith, by those who were not there either. Their response is no less unrelated to the actual event than is the response of the rebels and disbelievers. Neither of them succeeds in establishing genuine contact with the world of the *Shoa*.

Those of us who were not there must, before anything else, heed the responses of those who were, for theirs alone are the authentic ones. Many who were there lost their faith. I can understand them. A Hell fiercer than Dante's was their lot. I believe that God himself understands and does not hold their loss of faith against them. Such is my faith in God. Can I, therefore, adopt their attitude for myself and rebel and reject? I was not there myself. I am not Job. I am only his brother. I cannot reject because there were others, too, in the thousands, in the tens of thousands, who were there and did not lose their faith; who accepted what happened to them in awesome submission to the will of God. I, who was not there, cannot reject, because to reject would be a desecration of the sacrifice of the myriads who accepted their lot in faith. How dare I reject, if they accepted! Neither can I accept. I who was not there, because I was not there, dare not accept, dare not submit, because my brothers in their tens of thousands, who did go through that hell, did rebel and did reject. How dare I, who was not there, accept their superhuman suffering and submit to it in faith!

I stand in awe before the memory of the *k'doshim* who walked into the gas chambers with the Ani Ma'amin—I believe!—on their lips. How dare I question, if they did not question! I believe, because they believed. And I stand in awe before the *k'doshim*, before the memory of the untold suffering of innocent human beings who walked to the gas chambers without faith, because what was imposed upon them was more than man can endure. They could not believe any longer; and now I do not know how to believe, so well do I understand their disbelief. In fact, I find it easier to understand the loss of faith in the "Kz" than the faith preserved and affirmed. The faith affirmed was superhuman; the loss of faith— in the circumstances—human. Since I am only human, what is human is nearer to me than the superhuman. The faith is holy; but so, also, is the disbelief and the religious rebellion of the concentration camps holy. The disbelief was not intellectual but faith crushed, shattered, pulverized; and faith murdered a millionfold is holy disbelief. Those who were not there and, yet, readily accept the holocaust as the will of God that must not be questioned, desecrate the holy disbelief of those whose faith was murdered. And those who were not there, and yet join with self-assurance the rank of the disbelievers, desecrate the holy faith of the believers.

One may, perhaps, go even further and say: The pious believer who was not there but meekly submits, not to his own destruction, but to that of six million of his brethren, insults with his faith the faith of the concentration camps. The *k'doshim,* who affirmed their faith in the God of Israel in the light of the doom that surrounded them may well say to such an eager believer: "What do you know about believing, about having faith? How dare you submit into suffering that is not yours. Calm yourselves and be silent." But they, too, who were not there and yet declare from the housetops their disbelief in the God of Israel, insult the holy disbelief of the concentration camps. They who lost their faith there may well turn to our radical theologians, saying: "How dare you speak about loss of faith, what do you know about losing faith, you who have never known what we have known, who never experienced what we have experienced?" In the presence of the holy faith of the crematoria, the ready faith of those who were not there, is vulgarity. But the disbelief of the sophisticated intellectual in the midst of an affluent society—in the light of the holy disbelief of the crematoria—is obscenity.

We are not Job and we dare not speak and respond as if we were. We are only Job's brother. We must believe, because our brother Job believed; and we must question, because our brother Job so often could not believe any longer. This is not a comfortable situation; but it is our condition in this era after the holocaust. In it alone do we stand at the threshold to an adequate response to the *Shoa*—if there be one. It is from this threshold alone that the break in and the breakthrough must come. It must come without the desecration of the holy faith or of the holy loss of faith of the Jewish people in the European hell. And if there be no breakthrough, the honest thing is to remain at the threshold. If there is no answer, it is better to live without it than to find peace either in the sham of an insensitive faith or in the humbug of a disbelief entertained by people who have eaten their fill at the tables of a satiated society.

CHAPTER I

MAN AND THE HOLOCAUST

I. THE ACQUIESCENCE OF THE WEST

Since history is, first, man's responsibility, we should begin our examination by questioning and discussing man himself. Perhaps even more important than the question, Where was God? is, Where was Man? It is not our task to tell the story of mankind's behavior in view of the *hurban* (destruction) of European Jewry. Enough has been written about practically the whole of Europe gone mad with anti-Jewish barbarism. The Poles, the Lithuanians, the Ukranians, the Slovaks, the Hungarians, the Rumanians did not need much encouragement from the Germans. Many of them out-did the Germans in cruelty and inhumanity, if that was at all possible. Some of the French, the Dutch, the Czechs, were not far behind. Our main concern here is with the attitude of the free world, the Allies, the churches, and some of the neutral nations. Again, it is not our intention to tell the story. It has been told well by qualified authors. Books like *The Catholic Church and Nazi Germany,* by Guenter Lewy, and *While Six Million Died, A Chronicle of American Apathy,* by Arthur D. Morse, describe and document with frightening impact not only the apathy of the world in the face of the catastrophe, but its actual genocide-encouraging silence or even active moral sympathy with the gruesome facts of the devilish extermination of a people. Our concern is with the moral aspect of that attitude and its consequences for' the present human predicament. For this purpose we shall discuss some of the major features of the so-called "apathy" of the free world. In this connection I wish to acknowledge my indebtedness especially to the work of Morse, on whose excellent presentation of this dismal

7

story I chiefly rely. However, the conclusions we reach are also supported by the work of Lewy, as well as by the Hebrew memoirs of Rabbi M. D. Weissmandel, *Min Hamezar,* not to mention a great deal of other literature one has read in the course of the years.

1.

One often hears and reads of the apathy of the major governments among the Allies towards the Nazi-German crime against the Jewish people. The truth, however, is that it was not only apathy but often actual sabotaging of possible plans of rescue. There were two farcical conferences on refugees of Evian and of Bermuda, which proved to the Germans that the world was not prepared to lend a helping hand to the Jews. On the contrary, they served as actual encouragement to Nazi Germany to go ahead with its plans of extermination. In the earlier days of the war, the State Department in particular even made every possible effort to suppress information about the German barbarities for fear that this might increase public pressure to something positive to help the victims. Actually, there was little need to worry on that account. Morse reports the public-opinion poll taken by *Fortune* magazine in April 1939, after the dismemberment of Czechoslovakia, on the question of whether, as a member of the Congress, one would vote "yes" or "no" on a bill to open the doors of the United States to refugees from Europe beyond the limits of the immigration quota system. The answers were devastating: 83 percent said no, 8.3 percent were undecided, and only 8.7 percent said yes. As the editors of Fortune summarized it: An American tradition was put to the test and it was repudiated by a majority of nearly ten to one. Not only was the quota system never relaxed during the entire period of mass slaughter, but every possible administrative hurdle was erected before the would-be immigrant, so that only a small percentage of the alloted quota was ever used.

Perhaps the most shameful forms of active acquiescence of the American and the British governments in the Hitlerite plan of extermination were the *St. Louis* and *Struma* episodes. The story of both refugee ships has been repeated often. There is little doubt that the refusal of the British government to allow the *Struma* passengers to proceed to Palestine, and that of the Americans to provide even a temporary sanctuary to the *St. Louis* refugees of whom the great majority were holding U.S. immigration quota numbers entitling them to enter the U.S.A. within the near future, were actual death sentences. The passengers of the *Struma* duly perished; that the same fate did not immediately overtake those on the *St. Louis* was not the fault of the U.S.A. As their ship was approaching Germany on its return trip, Belgium, Holland, France, and Britain finally took pity on the doomed refugees and jointly found shelter for them in their respective territories. How many of them did perish ultimately when the Germans swept into Western Europe no one knows. Significant in the cases of the *Struma* and the *St. Louis* is the fact that both times mighty nations refused to help, not in the name of some universally valid principle, but in order to protect man-made rules and principles, like immigration quotas and the British policy on Palestine, reasons that had of course no moral authority in the face of such unprecedented humanitarian emergency. One should recall the reason why, for instance, an American secretary of state refused to grant asylum to people whose forced return to Germany meant certain death. Said he, with deep patriotic conviction: "I took an oath to protect the flag and obey the laws of my country and you are asking me to break those laws."[1] Is there much difference between such an argument and that of the Nazi war criminals at Nuremberg and after, who pleaded their oath to the Führer and their country! There may be a difference in degree, but none in kind.

It was not even possible to get an unequivocal official condemnation of the Nazi crimes against the Jews from the Allied governments. When, in 1940, news reached the outside world of the deportations, in most inhuman conditions, of tens of thousands of Jews from the Reich to questionable destinations in Poland, one assistant secretary of state submitted a memorandum to his department in which he stated that even if only 20 percent of the reports were true, it raised a problem that "ought to enlist our humanitarian interest. . . . we cannot be party to any ultimate arrangement which sanctions that kind of cruelty on an organized scale."[2] He was wrong. According to the answer he was given the mass murders were a domestic matter, completely within the jurisdiction of Germany; furthermore, since the publication of Hitler's

Mein Kampf, it had been known that "these poor people would be subjected to all kinds of improper treatment."[3] It appears it was the opinion of the State Department that one's "humanitarian interest" was sufficiently engaged by referring to the victims as "poor people." It showed where the American government's sympathies lay. Nothing more was required since what was happening was not more serious than "improper treatment" of whose eventual approach the world had been given due notice.

During the entire period of the genocide perpetrated on the Jewish people there was not a single united official condemnation by the Allies of the crime. The Moscow Declaration of 1943 that warned the war criminals made mention of numerous crimes, but not a word was mentioned about the Jews, who had been singled out for hatred, humiliation, and destruction by the Germans. Was this not an actual signal given to Germany to continue with its plans against the Jews?

Every attempt to rescue larger numbers of Jews—and there were such possibilities—was stifled, especially by the British foreign office because, in the words of an American ambassador, the foreign office was "concerned with the difficulties of disposing of any considerable number of Jews should they be rescued."[4] In view of the record, Arthur D. Morse's view is fully justified when he states: "The possibility of mass rescue threatened England's Palestine policies; the vision of Jews streaming to Palestine seemed to upset Whitehall more than the vision of Jews walking to their death in the gas chambers."[5] One might add only that not only was Whitehall more upset by such a vision, but so were most other governments of the world more upset by the vision of Jews finding even temporary refuge on their shores than by the vision of the gas chambers and crematoria.

However, not only did most of the nations resist opening the gates of their lands to rescue efforts, they even refused to undertake any kind of action that might have interfered with the smooth running of the daily death transports to the concentration camps in Poland. There were military reasons for not bombing the railway lines leading to Auschwitz and to the other camps. But surely, they could have been sabotaged by the underground and the resistance movements. In fact, the Jews themselves could have done it, had they been given an opportunity. At a time when 700,000 Jews were still alive in Hungary, hundreds of Palestinian Jews were waiting ready to be parachuted into that country. Their presence might have made all the difference in retarding and, perhaps, even preventing the extermination of Hungarian Jewry. It was also in the military interest of the Allies. It was rejected for political reasons: it would have implied a recognition of Palestinian Jewry as a partner in the Allied struggle. The camp and the railway lines were not bombed for military reasons; Jews were not allowed to help themselves for political reasons. M. D. Weissmandel, in *Min Hamezar,* tells how the Germans and their accomplices in Czechoslovakia and Hungary were wont to joke: The safest way to get vital military transports to the fronts was to put some Jews in them and write on cars in large letters: This is a Jew transport to an extermination camp. Thus it was sure not to be molested by the Allies. This is the most devastating moral condemnation of the attitude of the Allied powers to the Jewish catastrophe.

Most revealing of the mood of the times are the arguments used by the opponents of proposed senatorial resolution to admit twenty thousand children from Germany. Some maintained that the country would be flooded with foreigners who would try to run it differently than desired by "the old stock"; some, that what was intended was not really a refugee bill, since most of those to be admitted would be Jews; some saw in it a response to foreign nationalistic or racial groups. Most original was the claim of those who feared that if the United States of America were to admit the number of children suggested, it would no longer be able to guarantee to its own children their right to life, liberty, and the pursuits of happiness. The prospective young immigrants, under fourteen years of age, were described as "thousands of motherless, embittered, persecuted children of undesirable foreigners," potential leaders of revolt against the American form of government. They were also called potential Communists, of whom there were already too many of their kind trying to overthrow "our government." One sees the arguments were very much like those of the Nazis themselves, who considered every Jew, men, women and children, as a Communist criminal. In essence there was no difference between the murderers of these children and those who refused to save them. Can one think of a more hypocritical reason for not saving children from persecution and death than the one put forward by the American Legion that "it was traditional American policy that home life should be preserved and that the American Legion therefore strongly oppose the breaking up of families, which would be done by the proposed legislation"?[6] Obviously, in the minds of these people "the traditional American policy" was by far superior to the tradition of those cruel Jewish parents who were willing to part with their children rather than perish together with them in the bliss of family communion in the concentration camps (where, of course, in fact husbands and wives, parents and children were forcibly separated from each other). But this kind of Americanism was perhaps surpassed by that of Congressman Karl E. Mundt, who was against the relaxation of the immigration laws in order to save the Jewish victims of Nazi Germany because "it was not the American way to single one group for special consideration."[7] No American idea was safe from being used in the noble effort to make sure that as many Jews as possible would remain behind the walls of the Nazi fortress. The children's bill was defeated and the proud republic, whose vast territory had only recently been purloined from the Indians, was saved.

The Nazis had a comparatively easy time of it. There was great understanding evinced for their antisemitism the world over. After all, hatred and suspicion of the Jew were deeply rooted in the Christian civilization of the West. The venom had been spread for many centuries. What the world did not realize was that one cannot revive old slumbering hatreds and prejudices and render them respectable without debauching the moral foundations of an entire civilization. To what extent demoralization had engulfed the West may be gauged by comparing the attitudes of successive American governments toward pogroms and Jewish persecutions in Russia, Rumania, Turkey in the nineteenth and early twentieth century, with the forebearance toward Nazi Germany. In 1902, for instance, notwithstanding their persecution the position of the Jews in Rumania was idyllic compared with that of the Jews under the German yoke forty years later. Yet, an American government found it appropriate to protest to Rumania against her treatment of the Jews for the reason "that it could not be a tacit party to such an international wrong." The realization was still alive that to remain silent would make one a party to the wrong. Forty years later, in the presence of far greater wrongs, the conscience of the world had become insensitive to such considerations, and the nations became not only tacit parties, but, through their attitude of active refusal to help, active accomplices in the greatest crime in history. By that time, a high official in the State Department complained about the publicity that had been given to the fate of the Jew by "Jewish interests." [9] By then the fate of the Jew in the world had become, in the most democratic country in the world, purely a matter of Jewish interest. Whereas a generation before the United States government spoke up on behalf of the victims of persecution "in the name of humanity," now such matters, in the opinion of a high government official, had only "a remote humanitarian" interest for the general public and its representatives in Congress. [10] The Hitlerite demoralization of the West had reached such a stage that normal humanitarian dictates of man's conscience had lost their commanding quality. The degradation of the Western conscience is correctly reflected in the words of the Yiddish poet, Itzhak Katzenelson, whose life, with just a little less indifference, could easily have been saved: "Sure enough, the nations did not interfere, nor did they protest, nor shake their heads, nor did they warn the murderers, never a murmur. It was as if the leaders of the nations were afraid that the killings might stop." [11] He was not altogether right. In March 1944, there was a murmur from President Roosevelt and quite an audible one. Katzenelson never heard it. By the time the news might have reached the concentration camps he was dead, as were the overwhelming majority of his six million brothers and sisters. There were some high-minded individuals who fully understood what was at stake. One of them formulated the issue clearly in the case of the struggle for the admission of the children from Germany. It was, he said, "whether the American people have lost their ability to respond to such tragic situations as this one. If it turns out that we have lost that ability, it will mean that much of the soul has gone out of America." [12] He was right not only as regards the question of the children, but concerning

the more comprehensive issue of saving a helpless people condemned to extermination. Nor was the challenge addressed to
America alone, but to all the free nations. The soul had gone out,
not only of America, but out of the majority of the Western nations. A Jew, of course, familiar with the history of his nation
within the domain of Western civilization, might well be wondering
how much soul was ever present in that civilization.

2.

The wonder about the quality of the soul of the West is never
more justified than when one considers the official attitude of
Christianity toward the Nazi crime against the Jewish people. There
were some courageous spiritual leaders of Christianity that spoke
up strongly against the persecution. There were quite a few, in
the clergy in France and Holland who, at the risk of their own
lives, did their utmost to help the persecuted. Needless to say, in
relationship to the magnitude of the catastrophe all their magnificent efforts were only marginal. The situation demanded the
arousal of Christianity by an official policy of the churches to
protest, to condemn, and to save. But, in the words of Katzenelson,
from the churches in their official capacity there was no interference,
no head-shaking, never a murmur. There was no difference in this
regard between Catholics and Protestants. If we shall quote some
of the statements of the Catholic hierarchy, it is because they are
on record beside the equally eloquent silence of the Protestant
churches.

There is no need to waste many words on the churches in Germany and in occupied Poland, Slovakia, and Hungary. They are
below all possible criticism. They were actual accomplices of the
Nazis. G. Lewy provides us with a remarkably massive docu-
mentation. For instance, addressing a gathering of Catholic youth
in the Cathedral of Trier, Bishop Bornewasser had the following
encouraging words to say: "With raised heads and firm step we
have entered the new Reich and we are prepared to serve it with
all the might of our body and soul." [13] And so they did to the very
end. Another bishop could say, in the name of the church in
Germany, that the German bishops not only accepted and recog-

nized the new state but served it "with ardent love and with all
our strength." [14] A renowned theologian of Tübingen had the
original idea that National Socialism and Catholicism belonged
together as nature and grace. [15] The idea took root in the theology
of German Catholicism. In a Jesuit monthly, in which it was
stated that the "person of Hitler has become the symbol of the
faith of the German nation in its existence and future," the following revealing harmony was recognized between the swastika
and the Christian cross: "The symbol of nature [i.e., the swastika]
only finds its fulfillment and consummation in the symbol of grace
[i.e., the cross]." [16] Heil Hitler and Jesus! Should ever the story of
the German Protestant church during the Nazi era be written, it
will prove to have been even more shameful than that of the
Catholic. However, our concern here is mainly with the position
taken by the Vatican.

In 1942, the genocide committed on the Jewish people was well
under way. The personal representative of the American president
at the Vatican inquired of the Vatican secretary of state whether
the Pope had any suggestions as to a practical manner in which
the forces of civilized public opinion could be utilized in order
to prevent a continuation of these barbarities. [17] The reply to this
inquiry reveals the Vatican's acquiescing complicity in those barbarities. According to the Vatican secretary of state, reports on
the measures against the Jews did reach the Vatican, but it was
not possible to ascertain their veracity. Another cardinal spoke of
"a great Pope" in Rome, who had given "unmistakeable proofs of
a great and undiscriminating affection for all peoples," who however, "in order to avoid the slightest appearance of partiality,
imposed upon himself, in word and deed, the most delicate reserve." [18] What an agony it must have been for the great Pope to
have had to impose upon himself such delicate reserve in word
and deed, doing nothing and saying nothing, while six million
human beings who were not participants in the war, were being
butchered. He demonstrated for our generation that to be a silent
bystander when a crime is being committed is morally justifiable
as an act of delicate reserve for fear of appearing to be partial in
favor of the victim. When, today, in our large cities numerous

crimes are committed and are witnessed by people who yet would not intervene. let no one complain. These people are not necessarily insensitive to the plight of their fellow man. On the contrary! They may well have an "undiscriminating affection" for all men. But just because their affection is undiscriminating, they will do nothing that might give even the appearance of being partial on the side of the victim. Even as late as April 1944, when the fate of over four-hundred-thousand Hungarian Jews was at stake, the "great Pope" had still made strenuous efforts to preserve his impartiality. Hungary was essentially a Catholic country. The value of a strong stand taken by the Vatican would have been incalculable. In April 1944, the war Refugee Board, in a direct message to the Pope, asked his intervention in the form of threat of excommunication of the participants in the expulsion of the Jews to the death camps in Poland. A rather weak message was sent to the Regent of Hungary, which—although it contained no threat of spiritual punishment of any kind and was "characteristically evasive," [19] did have some beneficial results. Only that, by the time it was sent after a delay of two months, three hundred fifty thousand of those deported had been gassed.

By its attitude toward the fate of the Jewish people, the Vatican, as also the other churches, lost all claim to moral and spiritual leadership in the world. While, undoubtedly, political considerations played their part, it is hard to believe that politics alone was responsible for this utter failure to respond to what should have been elementary demands of a sane human conscience. There is sufficient evidence to believe that an ingrained theological anti-semitism that for long centuries had nourished Christianity and was responsible for a tradition of Christian inhumanity toward the Jew was ultimately responsible for the spiritual madness of encouraging acquiescence. M. D. Weissmandel, in his memoirs of his experiences in Slovakia, tells of two characteristic encounters with the Catholic hierarchy in that country. Among the German satellites there had been no puppet government more anxious to get rid of all the Jews than that of the Catholic priest Tisso in Slovakia. Shortly before Passover, 1942, one of the most respected rabbis in Slovakia approached the Archbishop Kametko[20] whom he had known from happier days, to influence his former private

secretary Tisso to prevent the expulsion of the Jews from his
country. The rabbi spoke of the threat of expulsion only. The
archbishop, however, with characteristic Christian love, decided
to enlighten him regarding the true fate that was awaiting the Jews
in Poland. These were his words: "This is no mere expulsion.
There—you will not die of hunger and pestilence; there—they will
slaughter you all, old and young, women and children, in one day.
This is your punishment for the death of our Redeemer. There is
only one hope for you—to convert all to our religion. Then I
shall effect the annulling of this decree." [21] As a result of Christian
theology, teaching, and tradition, the feeling among Christians was
widespread that the Jews were receiving what was due them. No
one expressed it more succinctly than the papal nuncio in Slovakia.
In the fall of 1944, Weissmandel together with his family and
hundreds of other Jews had been put into a temporary camp prior to
their deportation to Auschwitz. Weissmandel escaped and suc-
ceeded in making his way to the residence of the papal nuncio.
He described to his eminence the conditions of the families in the
camp and asked for his immediate intervention with Tisso. Upon
his urging, he received the following answer:

"This, being a Sunday, is a holy day for us. Neither I nor Father
Tisso occupy ourselves with profane matters on this day."

Upon Weissmandel's wondering how the blood of infants and
children could be considered a profane matter, he was taught a
significant chapter in Christian theology. He was told:

"There is no innocent blood of Jewish children in the world.
All Jewish blood is guilty. You have to die. This is the punishment
that has been awaiting you because of that sin" (meaning the death
of Jesus). [22] One wonders whether in the entire history of the
human race the concept of holiness has ever been more degraded
and desecrated than in the mouth of that papal nuncio. He was
on that, for him, holy day repeating with deep religious conviction
the Hitlerite faith that all Jews are guilty. Hitler believed in it on
racial grounds, the archbishop and the papal nuncio, for theological
reasons. In practice it amounted to the same thing: death to all
Jews. Not all Christians felt that way, but many in high offices in
the churches did. The deicide accusation through the ages did its
murderous work in the Christian subconscious making Christianity,

in many cases, an active accomplice in the Nazi crime and, in most cases, "a tacit party to the barbarities."

Arnold J. Toynbee, in his *A Story of History,* discussing the significance of Nazi Germany has the following to say:

A Western nation, which for good or evil, had played so central a part in Western history since the first emergence of a nascent Western Civilization out of a post-Hellenic interregnum, could hardly have committed these flagrant crimes if the same criminality had not been festering foully below the surface of life in the Western world's non-German provinces. The twentieth-century German psyche was like one of those convex mirrors in which a gazer learns to read the character printed on his own countenance through seeing the salient features exaggerated in a revealing caricature. If a twentieth-century Germany was a monster, then, by the same token, a twentieth-century Western Civilization was a Frankenstein guilty of having been the author of this German monster's being.[23]

This evaluation of the relationship between Nazi-Germany and Western civilization is well born out by the attitude of Western civilization to Nazi Germany's genocide. The apathy, the toleration, the tacit encouragement, the "inpartiality" were only possible because indeed, in essence if not in degree, "the same kind of criminality had been festering foully below the surface of life in the Western world." The guilt of Germany is the guilt of the West. The fall of Germany is the fall of the West. Not only six million Jews perished in the holocaust. In it, Western civilization lost its every claim to dignity and respect. Since the days of the gas chambers and crematoria, either something entirely new will arise over the spiritual ruins of the West or there is no future for man in this nuclear age.

A THEOLOGY OF INTOLERANCE

Needless to say, Western civilization has been essentially Christian civilization. From the point of view of the spirit, the holocaust has been a Christian catastrophe much more than a Jewish one. There is little doubt that without the insults, humiliations, and degradations heaped by Christianity upon Judaism and the Jewish people through many centuries; without the ceaseless oppression, discrimination, expulsions, pogroms, massacres, practised in Christian lands on the Jews, the holocaust would not have been possible. The rich resources of international hatred, demoralization, and indifference, without which this greatest crime in history could not have been perpetrated, would simply not have been available for the originally rather small group of Nazis to draw on. Hitler was right when, in his meeting with two high dignitaries of the Church in April 1933, he declared that "he merely wanted to do more effectively what the Church had attempted to accomplish for so long." He maintained that what he was doing about the Jews was service to a common cause.[24] And he could not be contradicted.

Of late there has been some measure of realization of the Christian guilt in the history of Jewish martryrdom on the part of some Christians as is such a subjectively honest attempt to introduce some missing pages into Christian history books as Father Flannery's work, *The Anguish of the Jews.*[25]

As to *The Anguish of the Jews,* I can do no better, perhaps, than introduce here what I have written in my review of the book in another place.[26]

There is no doubt that Flannery, striving for objectivity, was convinced that he let the facts speak for themselves. But no one, writing history, can ever just let facts speak for themselves. The facts are always too numerous and one must always select from among them. The historian selects; he organizes his material and presents it; but this is interpretation. *The Anguish of the Jews* is a Christian interpretation of twenty-three centuries of antisemitism. Notwithstanding the author's unquestionable intellectual honesty, the final outcome of his work is Christian apologetics. While the Christian share in the anguish of the Jews is mitigated by "explanation," the Jewish responsibility for it is greatly magnified. True, what remains of history, even in the opinion of the author, is still a terrible indictment, if not of Christianity, certainly of Christendom.

The author assumes a form of co-responsibility of Christian and Jew for the horrors of Jewish persecution through the centuries. One must, however, take objection to a position which is formulated in the opening remarks of the presentation in the statement: "Our history is a tale of horror and scandal, involving both the Church and the Synagogue." In view of the fact that, even in the opinion of Flannery, the Jewish responsibility is dwarfed by the

Christian share of the guilt,[27] the statement is utterly misleading.
While there were acts of violence committed by Jews against
Christians in the early centuries, they were not the rule but the
exception, they were of a very limited local nature, and they soon
were chiefly retaliatory in character. What, however, is lacking in
Judaism even in the earliest time of the Judeo-Christian conflict,
is a Jewish ideology of Christian-hatred, as there exists a very
theology of the Christian hatred of the Jew. Whereas the hatred
for Judaism and the Jew is amply illustrated in the writings of the
Church Fathers and a host of the princes of the Church through
the ages, only in the same antisemitic writings do we find testimony
to a similar Jewish anti-Christian animosity. Since the Jewish
sources are free of them, it is more than likely that the Christian
authors were projecting their own hatred of the Jew onto the
Jew, ascribing to him the same kind of feelings towards Christians
and Christianity that they themselves felt towards Jews and Judaism. The prayer against the *minim* is not a very laudable one; it
becomes understandable if one sees it in its proper historical context. Even if one should agree with Marcel Simon's conclusion
that by *minim* were meant all Christians, how mild is such an
expression of animosity compared to the venomous fulminations
of a Gregory of Nyssa or Chrysostom—if one had to wait till the
twentieth century in order to establish its meaning. It is a pity that
Flannery relies for his knowledge of Judaism on secondary sources,
on the interpretation of interpreters. The fact is that the statement
that Judaism considers, or even considered, Christianity "the greatest apostasy from Judaism" is theologically senseless. No gentile
can ever be guilty of apostasy from Judaism. Judaism has never
been considered obligatory on gentiles. Therefore, if *minim* meant
Christians, it could never have meant "all Christians," gentile
Christians, but only apostate Jews. How innocuous are the few
and far between derogatory references to Christians and Christianity in Talmud and Midrash compared to the overrich anti-Jewish
venom which one finds in the works of the Church Fathers and
their successors in the bishoprics and the monasteries!

Explaining the horror and the scandal in which the Church was
involved, Flannery distinguishes between Scriptures and Christian
doctrine on the one hand, and pastoral zeal on the other. All

responsibility for Christian antisemitism is apportioned to the latter.[28] One wonders whether such a neat distinction is possible. According to the doctrine, the Church protected "the basic rights" of the Jews. That sounds good. The truth, however, is that this "protection" never permitted that the Jew be treated as an equal. In keeping with the doctrine, the Jew was reduced by legislation to an inferior status. And woe unto the secular ruler who dared treat them with ordinary human decency. The "basic rights" were jealously guarded by bishops and popes to reflect the fallen nature of the Jew. In vain does Flannery refer to the Pauline doctrine regarding the Jews as the true Christian position. Even this doctrine considers the Jews a fallen and faithless people to whom charity is due "for the sake of their fathers." But charity asked for a people that in the same breath is called fallen and faithless has little effect in history. It is more doctrinaire than real. In one place, in order to mitigate the fairly inhuman outpourings of hate of a Chrysostom, the author speaks of theological antisemitism. It would seem to us that it is the hatred that is real and the charity that is theological. This alone explains why Christendom so seldom followed the Pauline doctrine and why the legislative "protection" of "basic rights" was seldom respected. The doctrine demanded that the code be heeded in principle; the hatred ensured that it would be ignored in practice.[29]

Flannery allocates the responsibility for the massacres during the crusades to the *pauperes,* "the poor men," who were a form of advance guard "for the more disciplined crusaders under Godfrey." Yet, on the same page[30] he has to record that when these more disciplined soldiers of Godfrey reached Jerusalem, they "found the Jews assembled in a synagogue and set it ablaze." For centuries, the burning alive of Jews, and even of entire congregations, was a familiar feature of what Flannery calls "the horror and the scandal involving both the Church and the Synagogue." Variously, he maintains that "the massacres were clearly mob actions, reinforced by religious fanaticism." The truth is that the mob was a Christian mob; it acted like a mob because it was continually fed on venomous hatred against everything Jewish. The Christian populace acted as was to be expected of the disciples of a Gregory of Nyssa, of a Chrysostom, of an Agobard, an Amulo,

an Innocent III, a Capistrano, a Paul IV, not to mention the
lesser luminaries among the priests and the monks who followed
in their footsteps. What chance did the Pauline doctrine of tolerance
have if even Gregory the Great, the most just among the popes, in
his homilies and commentaries described the Jews in a manner
"more close to a fourth-century image of the Jew as a dark, blind,
and perverse unbeliever"![31] The mobs were the least responsible
for the massacres; the moral responsibility must be placed squarely
on the shoulders of those who taught them, guided them, led them.

A word must be said here about the antisemitism of the Christian Scriptures. Our author dismisses the subject rather lightly.
In our opinion, the theological interpretation of a term like "the
synagogue of Satan" (Revelation 2:9) is beside the point in a
history of antisemitism. The important question is how the phrase
was understood by the populace. That the antisemitism of John
is "only apparent"[32] is irrelevant. The fact is that the contemporary
Jew was a follower of the Pharisaic interpretation of Judaism and
was identified with those of whom it was said that they were of
their "father the devil, and the lusts of your father ye will do. He
was a murderer from the beginning. . . ." (John 8:44). No matter
what the deeper theological meaning of the Gospel references to
the Jews may be, for centuries myriads of Christians were reading:
"Woe unto you, scribes and Pharisees, hypocrites . . . ye serpents,
ye generation of vipers, how can you escape the damnation of
hell?" (Matthew 23:33), and were thinking of their Jewish neighbors. They were continually admonished so to identify the Jew
by Church Fathers, bishops, priests, monks. It would seem to us
that Flannery is wrong in maintaining that the picture of the Jew
as the devil was created only in the fourth century. In fact, Gregory
of Nyssa, Chrysostom, and the innumerable others were only
playing variations on themes already clearly developed in the
Gospels. No matter what the esoteric theological interpretation of
these passages of wrath against Jews in the Gospels may be, in
their historic effect they represent a literature of hatred, the
parallel to which one will find only in the writings of twentieth-
century Nazism and present-day Soviet Russia. And indeed, the
most scurrilous of all Nazi antisemitic publications, Streicher's *Der
Stürmer,* drew heavily on the Gospel passages about the Jews for

support. As a young student in Berlin, I was introduced to the New Testament by the showcases in which *Der Stürmer* was so widely displayed in the streets of the German capital.

What of the Jewish involvement in the horror and the scandal? The author sees it in a number of areas. We hear him repeat again and again that, notwithstanding their utter political helplessness, Jews were nevertheless "powerful and aggressive enough to alarm the Church." Their power and aggressiveness consisted in Judaizing and proselytizing. In other words, they represented a spiritual challenge to Christianity. It may very well be that Judaism did attract numerous converts at certain periods in history. The author makes, however, a very weak case in proving "aggressiveness" in proselytizing. Judaism, by its very nature, is not a missionary religion. Be that as it may, the Christian response to the conversion of an emperor's chaplain to Judaism with oppression and per- secution, should not be put in the Jewish debit scale. Then, of course, Jews were usurers, involuntarily so—as the author acknowl- edges it. No doubt Jewish usurers "often plied their trade impru- dently." [33] Rich Jews were often foolishly ostentatious. Jews often reacted to massacres, expulsions, rapine, and plunder, with hatred for their torturers and murderers, and more often, with well deserved contempt. At times, they were themselves intolerant. In short, they were only human. One might also say that their chief guilt was that they were involved in existence and history. However, our author's greatest mistake is that he imagines that he wrote the history of twenty-three centuries of antisemitism. Antisemitism existed in Greece and Rome; Voltaire and some philosophers of the En- lightenment were also antisemites. There is antisemitism in America today. The oppression, the expulsions, the massacres and pogroms which were inflicted upon Jews in Christian lands through many centuries right up to our own age, was not antisemitism, but inhumanity and barbarism unequaled in the annals of men. Jews have, at times, been guilty of being only human. However, their long martyrdom was not due to their human faults, but to the inhumanity of their enemies.

We sympathize with the author's attempt to absolve Christianity from all share in the Nazi crime against the Jews. Yet, we believe that the matter cannot be so easily disposed of. The conscious motivation of a pagan antisemitism is of course different from the conscious motivation of its Christian counterpart. But the conscious motivation is secondary when one appeals to such deep-rooted an emotion as hatred. No one knew this better than Hitler himself. He spoke the most condemning truth about nineteen centuries of Christian civilization when he said to Rauschning: "You will see how little time we shall need in order to upset the ideas and criteria of the whole world, simply and purely *(sic)* attacking Judaism. It is beyond question the most important weapon in my propaganda arsenal."[34] How right he was! The Christian bequest of eighteen centuries of Jew-hatred made the path of Hitler a comparatively easy one. A pagan Nazism was making effective use of a replete reservoir of Christian hatred of the Jew. In a number of passages[35] Flannery attributes Christian antisemitism of the early centuries to the influx of the Roman middle class into the church. It was the pagan antisemitism living on in Christian guise. If this may be said of pagan antisemitism, which—according to the author's own testimony[36] "remained primarily literary and cultural, the handiwork of nativistic intellectuals," how much more to the point is it to say that Nazi antisemitism was so successful because it was essentially a carryover from the Christian era under pagan guise! The "explanations" of Flannery, are, however, in essence irrelevant because we see the great spiritual tragedy of Christianity in the fact that with respect to antisemitism, nineteen centuries of Christianity made no difference. On the contrary! It was during the Christian era that antisemitism became inhumanly barbarous.

We agree wholeheartedly with Flannery's warning against the temptation for the Jew "to nurture a grievance against the progeny of his persecutors and indulge in some degree of anti-Christianity."[37] It would, however, be foolhardy of the Jew not to look critically at a culture and a civilization that is responsible for so much Jewish suffering as is the Christian. Since the tree is to be judged by its fruits, the standards and values of this religion and civilization have become questionable. Christianity never really presented a serious spiritual challenge for the Jew. In view of the Christian performance through the ages, Christianity has never been as dead an option for the Jew as it is today.

As to Jewish-Christian relations in the future, they can be ethical, if they are based on an honest agreement to disagree on basic principles of religious faith and dogma. For the Jew the adoption of such an attitude toward Christians and Christianity is Jewish. By its very essence, Judaism is not a missionary religion. In keeping with fundamental Jewish teaching, in the century of the Second Crusade, Rabbenu Tam formulated the idea unequivocally that "the intention of the Christian is directed to the Creator of heaven and earth." Christianity is not to be considered an idolatry. Even though Christians associate another person with the Godhead, this is not forbidden for non-Jews.³⁸ Can Christianity reciprocate with the same kind of theological tolerance? Flannery finds the questionable attitude of the Church in order on the ground that the Church considers "herself . . . the solicitous mother, fearful for the health of her family, desirous of its growth, saddened by the defection of her eldest." ³⁹ This, in our opinion, is an attitude of conceit and pride. Anyone is free to believe what he pleases, as long as his belief effects only himself. But our beliefs and dogmas must not detrimentally effect other people. We are entitled to sacrifice our very lives to what we believe, but it is immoral to sacrifice one iota of the human happiness of others to our own religious conviction. Flannery ought to realize that what may seem simple from the Christian point of view may be more than questionable to the conscience of a non-Christian. A non-Christian will consider even the Pauline doctrine concerning the Jews inadequate. Even according to this doctrine, which for Flannery is the true expression of Church teaching, Jews, "are enemies for your sakes," "the branches that were broken off because of unbelief"; they are the faithless sinners, but "they are beloved for their fathers' sake." Outside the realm of Christianity, a form of charity based on such theological premises is ethically objectionable. One cannot help wondering whether, after all is said, Christianity is not by its fundamental doctrine bound to an anti-Judaic and anti-Jewish stance in history. Of course, such a stance disintegrates the moral integrity of our entire civilization.

What are we to glean from the Vatican Council's schema on the Jews? and that the highest instance in world Catholicism, the

Vatican Council,[40] went as far as to declare that the Jews, after all, are not to be considered a people accursed by God; they are not collectively guilty for the death of Jesus? Some people might consider this quite significant. However, Jews should not be impressed. Having persecuted them for centuries, the Church is now kind enough to say that the Jews are not altogether guilty. It is difficult to have much respect for such a declaration. It is more important, however, to say a few words on the rather ambiguous withdrawal of the deicide accusation.

As Jews, we are not a bit interested in the Christian preoccupation with the question of who killed Jesus. Innumerable good people have been killed in the course of history, hundreds of thousands among the noblest and most innocent, in Christian lands. But Jesus was a god! Yes, for Christians. Now anyone should be free to believe in any kind of a god. But it is sheer impudence to demand that others share one's own faith. To judge others in the light of one's own dogmas is barbarous. To persecute them because they dare believe differently from oneself is inhuman. Never in the entire history of the human race was a concept conceived to justify as much inhumanity as that of the deicide accusation against the Jewish people! Deicide is Christianity's shame. It will not be erased from the record until full confession and atonement are made for it.

There was one saintly Christian who understood this, Pope John XXIII. Before his death, he composed the following prayer, to be read in all Catholic churches. He called it, *Act of Reparation:*

> We are conscious today that many centuries of blindness have cloaked our eyes so that we can no longer see the beauty of Thy chosen people, nor recognize in their faces the features of our privileged brethren. We realize that the mark of Cain stands on our foreheads. Across the centuries our Brother Abel has lain in blood which we drew or shed tears we caused forgetting Thy love. Forgive us for the curse we falsely attached to their name as Jews. Forgive us for crucifying Thee a second time in their flesh. For we knew not what we did. . . .[41]

Pope John died before he could introduce his prayer into the liturgy. There is nothing of his spirit present in the Vatican Schema on the Jews. The prayer itself lies buried in the archives of the Vatican. On the day on which it will be unearthed and its contents integrated into the Christian conscience, there will be hope for the Spirit of God in Christendom.

The Uniformed Heart

1.

When, at the close of the Second World War, mankind's unbelieving eyes were compelled to acknowledge that the greatest crime in history actually took place during the twentieth century, no one could have imagined that in a decade or two attempts would be made to point an accusing finger at the victims themselves. It is a sad commentary on the conscience of man that for some time now the accusations against the Jewish martyrs have become almost louder than those against Nazi Germany. To find the victims guilty seems to be psychologically more satisfying to some people than to delve into the monstrosity of the crime committed against them. According to these theories, the victims themselves share in the guilt of a widely nazified Europe. They went like sheep to the slaughter. They should have resisted in their millions. Instead, at the behest of their leaders, they even cooperated with their enemies in their own destruction. This description of Jews, of course, does not agree with what we have seen of Jewish performance in the war of Israeli independence, only a few years after Auschwitz, when a small army, ill-equipped and ill-prepared for war, more than held its own against numerous invading armies that for years were preparing freely just for such an occasion. One would have thought that since then, and in the light of the pursuant history of the Jewish state, the cowardice hypothesis dubbed on to the Jews would have become untenable. The "vested interest" in the cowardice theory is so deep-reaching that in order to give it the shine of respectability the idea of two Jewries has been conceived: the one cowardly, the Jewry of the diaspora, the other, heroic, the Jewry of the State of Israel.[42] In a significant essay, an Israeli writer, K. Shabbetai, himself a survivor of concentration camps, shows convincingly how unfounded the hypothesis of the two Jewries is.[43] Shabbetai points to the courage of the Jewish partisans; to the numerous Jews who escaped the German march to the east and were recruited into the Red Army, who displayed great bravery and self-sacrifice as fighters and soldiers. They were the Jews from Vilno and Kovno, Kiev and Bialystok, among them quite a few escapees from the ghettos and the concentration camps. The

so-called Lithuanian Division of the Red Army, which was organized in 1941, consisted of eighty-five percent of Lithuanian
Jews, all refugees from Kovno, Vilno, Ponivezh and Shavli. This
division fought with distinction; the great majority of its members
fell fighting. Again, many of the physically broken survivors of
the camps shied away from no risk after the war to reach the
land of Israel, defying the British navy and Arab bullets. These
broken remnants were the heroes of "Aliya Beth," the illegal immigration to Israel, symbolically immortalized in *Exodus 1947*. The
very same diaspora Jews were in the forefront of the fighters for
Israel's independence and its defenders, performing no less bravely
than their sabra brothers. The two-Jewries hypothesis is a figment
of the imagination. The same Jews who, in the ghettos and the
death camps, went "like sheep to the slaughter" were bold, imagi-
native, resourceful, and heroic, once they found themselves outside
the iron grip of the German monster.

The flimsy hypothesis of two Jewries is an evasion of the true
issue. Shabbetai is correct in maintaining that the real problem
derives from the fact that in the one case the same people, apparently, went to their death without resistance, whereas in the
other they behaved with courage and heroism. He who does not
see it this way misses the problem completely. But in order to
understand the lack of Jewish resistance in so many cases, one
must compare the Jewish behavior with that of the gentiles in
similar situations. The facts mustered by Shabbetai are most im-
pressive. In addition to the Jews, there were about five million
non-Jews in German concentration and forced-labor camps. All
the nations of Europe were represented among the inmates. Yet,
there was no rebellion, no self-defense among them. It is true that
the conditions in the gentile camps were not as desperate as those
in the Jewish death camps. Yet, they were humiliating and degrading enough not to be endured by self-respecting people. Shabbetai quotes from the report of the American Third Army, which
describes the Flossenburg Concentration Camp as a "death fac-
tory." Starvation, brutality, medical neglect, exposure to freezing
cold, inducement of suicide by the prisoners, shooting and hanging
were the methods of extermination practiced in the camp. "Prisoners were murdered arbitrarily at the whim of their murderers.

All this was done to gentiles," comments Shabbetai. Yet, they never rebelled; they endured it like sheep. A most striking illustration of the point Shabbetai is making is the plight of the Russian prisoners of war, who perished in the German camps. Fifty thousand Soviet soldiers are buried in the mass grave at Bergen-Belsen. They all perished in a manner very similar to the Jewish martyrs. It should be noted that this number represents a small percentage of all the Soviet soldiers, prisoners of war, who perished in the German camps. Shabbetai quotes from a letter of Alfred Rosenberg, dated February 28, 1942, to Wilhelm Keitel, chief of the German General Staff, who wrote: "Of the 3,300,000 Russian prisoners of war, only a few hundred thousands remain today who are fit to work. Most of them died of hunger or froze to death. Thousands more were killed by typhus. Often the prisoners were shot in full view of the terrified civilian population, and their bodies left lying on the roads, when they lacked the strength to continue marching."

Polish intellectuals and army officers were murdered by the Germans. They offered no resistance. The nine thousand Polish officers massacred at Katyn offered no resistance. The examples are numerous. They all go to prove Shabbetai's thesis that resistance and rebellions have their own laws, whose functioning depends on political, strategic, social, and psychological conditions. If the conditions required are extant, people will resist and rebel; if not, they will not, they cannot. There is no rebellion after defeat: no rebellion as long as the enemy marches from victory to victory. The partisan movement along the eastern front did not really start until after the German defeat at Stalingrad. The Polish underground was organized soon after Poland's defeat. It had at its disposal the service of well-trained army officers, soldiers, weapons, funds, foreign support. Yet, for years its main function was to smuggle people out of Poland. In the meantime, Polish intellectuals, scientists, officers, leading citizens were being murdered or sent to concentration camps. But the Polish underground did not budge and people accepted their fate meekly. It took nearly five years after the collapse before the Warsaw revolt took place. And it happened after Stalingrad, after the overthrow of Mussolini, after the Allied landing in France, and at a time when the Russian armies were standing practically at the gate of Warsaw. Even revolt fears terror, even revolt needs hope. It must have a place to organize weapons, an avenue of possible escape or retreat.

These were laws operative all across German-occupied Europe. Millions of gentile people, oppressed and humiliated, exploited and massacred accepted their plight without resistance, until the required favorable conditions for a revolt arose. The Jews, however, were in an infinitely weaker and more exposed situation than all the other oppressed people of Europe. There were millions of them. But they were not an organized nation, living in their own homeland. They lived scattered in towns and cities all across Europe, separated and isolated from each other by national frontiers. Once the German armies moved into a country, even the inner structure of a Jewry was shattered. Whenever the German armies marched, the Jew lost his status as a human being. There were no laws protecting his elementary rights of existence. His former homeland was turned into his prison, surrounded not only by Nazi inhumanity, but also the brutality of the indigenous populations, the Poles, the Ukrainians, the Lithuanians, the Latvians, the Hungarians, the Rumanians, practically the whole of Europe gone mad with hatred and murder. Trapped was not an army trained for war, not people with a long tradition of warlike virtues; but men, women, and children, completely unprepared for such an emergency. Any possibility of organized resistance by the people in their vast masses was out of the question. There was no national leadership because there could not have been. Every community, and practically every individual Jew, had to face the limitless ferocity of the enemy in isolation. Especially in the Eastern European countries, where the large concentration of Jews was found, the enemy was—as far as the Jews were concerned—an almost completely nazified Europe. Those who were considering sporadic acts of resistance, which alone were possible, had to take into account the terrible consequences of collective punishment, which was employed by the Germans. Was it morally right to kill an S.S. man if, as a consequence, hundreds and even thousands of men, women, and children would perish immediately? All the available documents show that all those who did consider resistance were mostly unable to act because, for moral reasons, they could not disregard the collective punishment that would follow. Another aspect of the problem which has to be borne in mind, is convincingly discussed by Hannah Arendt.[44] The question was raised at the Eichman trial: "Why didn't you revolt and charge and attack?" Like Shabbetai, she points out how ill-taken the question was, "for no non-Jewish group or people had behaved differently." One could easily have found the answer to the question by letting one's imagination dwell on those Dutch Jews who were arrested as a reprisal for an attack on a German security police detachment in the old Jewish quarter of Amsterdam.

Four hundred and thirty Jews were arrested in reprisal and they were literally tortured to death, first in Buchenwald and then in the Austrian camp of Mauthausen. For months on end they died a thousand deaths, and every single one of them would have envied his brethren in Auschwitz and even in Riga and Minsk. There exist many things considerably worse than death, and the S.S. saw to it that none of them was ever very far from their victims' minds and imagination.

For a long period Jews could not imagine that the reports from the crematoria could be true, that any people could conceive the monstrous plan of ruthlessly exterminating another people. This disbelief was encouraged by the Nazi technique of making false promises, of creating confusion among the people, of cleverly hiding the intended terminal of the long trains that carried their terrible load all across Europe. Once in a concentration camp, ultimate despair and hopelessness descended upon the victims. From the psychological point of view one should not overlook the fact that in the ghettos and the camps there was something worse than death, i.e., life. For innumerable people, death was the redeemer. That so many went to their death "like sheep" because of disgust with what life had become was no cowardice but the most radical condemnation of a civilization in the midst of which such degradation of existence was possible. Then again, people can be broken by the kind of bestiality to which millions of Jews have been subjected, broken to such an extent that the idea of resistance cannot occur to them, not because of fear of death, but because of complete loss of sensitivity to their condition. To be shattered by superhuman inhumanity is not identical with cowardice.

Bearing in mind all relevant circumstances, one is inclined to agree with Shabbetai, who sums up his analysis in the following words:

The truth is that the question about going like sheep to the slaughter should be precisely reversed. Instead of asking: "Why did they not revolt?", or "Why did revolt begin so late, and why was resistance so weak?", we should ask, "If each circumstance separately and all together were against us, against the faintest possibility of self-defense, if entire powerful armies fell before the enemy, if the foreign enemy and the local one joined forces to obliterate us from the face of the earth, if we felt God and man had conspired to exterminate us; if our minds and hearts were paralyzed by starvation, confusion and shock, if army officers, commissars, and trained soldiers went to their death without a word—how, then, did it happen that our people, in spite of everything, retained sufficient strength, faith and will power to stand up to the enemy the way we did? How did it happen that, against all reasonable expectation, underground resistance movements were organized in the ghettoes, and acts of revolt did occur there? From what rock was this nation hewn? [45]

Even a random perusal of some of the available records will show how well-taken Shabbetai's point is. We are familiar with the Warsaw Ghetto revolt. But there were revolts and resistance in other ghettos and in numerous Jewish communities. Jews resisted hopelessly and fought back practically with bare fists at Vilno, Bialystok, Lemberg, Cracow, Bendin, Radin, Brody, Kletzk, Tarnow, Grodno, and in numerous other places. [46] There were revolts in the concentration camps at Treblinka, Auschwitz, Sobibor. [47] How many acts of organized rebellion remain unknown because all participants and all witnesses perished? By the mere chance of a letter handed to a Polish worker, we know of the burning of the camp at Kunin by the Jewish inmates. They all perished. The last Jews in the camp at Shavnia fell, without weapons, upon their guards. [48] Most of them were shot in the uneven combat. There was also a vast Jewish partisan movement. It was not easy for a Jew to run away from the Ghetto, and almost impossible to escape from a concentration camp. If he did succeed in escaping, it was not easy to reach the woods. One was hunted by the Germans and the local police and in most cases, risked the danger of being betrayed by the local population. Once in the woods, one could easily be killed by the antisemitic Polish partisans themselves. In most cases, one could join a more friendly partisan group, if one came with a weapon and without any family, wife, or child. Notwithstanding all the difficulties, there were numerous Jewish partisan bands in many parts of Eastern Europe, fighting and harassing the Germans with courage and heroism. Both in the Ghettos and the camps, acts of individual heroism and self-sacrifice were numberless. It would be futile to attempt to list them here. The roll of Jewish heroes whose names have been preserved, is endless. Even more numerous were the nameless heroes of hopeless resistance, the many "unknown soldiers" of this terrible struggle.

2.

However, there was also another type of courage and heroism extant in the ghettos and the death camps that can hardly be appreciated by the standards and value concepts of a culture that is ultimately responsible for Auschwitz, i.e., courage and heroism in its specifically Jewish expression, that of _kiddush haShem,_ the sanctification of the Divine Name, which we shall yet discuss in depth. Again, the recorded cases are numberless. Let us point only to a few. The Jews of Pristik were assembled in the marketplace. The infamous selection took place. An old woman of eighty, "the mother-in-law of David Moses Epstein" was among them, her head covered in the traditional religious manner. With a stick an S.S. man removed her head cover, which fell to the ground. The old woman bent down to pick it up. It was against the regulations. She was beaten, but she picked up her kerchief and covered her head. Once again, and in the same manner, her head was uncovered. Once again, she bent down, once again she was beaten. She remained unperturbed; picked up the kerchief and covered her head. In the end, the S.S. won.[40] An eyewitness tells of the following incident at Maidanek. A young woman of about twenty-six is led out to be hanged in the presence of the other inmates. Together with her sister she ran away from the airport at Lublin, where they were put to work. The sister managed to escape; but she was caught. It was a beautiful day in May. The gallows were set up at the center of the commando square, the victim and the hangman

standing beside it. The hangman started to question her: "Who
helped you to get away?" Her answer was: "A Jewess does not
betray those who tried to help her." "Don't you see how everybody
laughs at you!" said the German. "You are beautiful. One word
could save you. And the world is delightful." "Today you laugh,
tomorrow you will be laughed at!" were her last words.[50] How
right was Ringelblum when he wrote: "The story of the Jewish
woman will be a glorious page in the history of Jewry during the
present war."[51] It was true not only at Warsaw, but in all the other
ghettos, as well as in the concentration camps.

K. Shabbetai tells the typical story of Arye Sheftel. "He was a
teacher, a member of the Vilno underground, who now lives in
Israel. Sheftel's wife, a professional bacteriologist, had friends
among the Polish doctors in Vilno. They in turn had connections
with the Polish Nationalist Partisans, the A.K. (Armia Krajowa),
and suggested to her that the organization would probably accept
her, as well as her husband and son. But Arye Sheftel refused to
join the A.K. because he knew they were sworn enemies of the
Jews, and had themselves put Jews to death. However, he asked
his wife and son to join them, but Mrs. Sheftel refused to leave her
husband in order to save herself. Later, when the members of the
underground in the Vilno ghetto established connections with the
partisans and had a small chance of sending their people there,
Arye Sheftel was one of those who was offered an opportunity to
escape to the woods. The underground made one condition, however; he would have to go alone, without his wife and child. Now
it was the husband's turn to refuse to leave his family. Cases
similar to this occurred frequently in the ghettos."[52] Let us recall
the case of Dr. Janos Korczak, an outstanding educator and the
head of the orphanage in the Warsaw Ghetto. When the children
were taken away, he and his aides insisted on going along with
the children in the full knowledge of what was awaiting them.[53]
Or think of the case of the three last rabbis of Warsaw, Rabbi
Menahem Zemba, Rabbi Shimshon Stockhammer, and Rabbi David
Schapiro. The days of the ghetto were numbered. For some mysterious reason, the Catholic hierarchy of Poland underwent something
of a change of heart and decided to lend a hand in saving the last
remaining rabbis of Warsaw. The rabbis were asked to decide

whether they were willing to accept the offer to be smuggled out of the ghetto. They met to consider the proposal. For a long time no one spoke. Finally Rabbi Schapiro interrupted the silence and said:

I am the youngest and therefore what I have to say has no obligatory character for you. We know well that we can no longer help them in any way. However, merely by being with them, by not leaving them, we encourage them and strengthen them. It is the last possible encouragement that we can still give to the last Jews. I simply don't have the strength to leave these unfortunate people.

They refused to be saved. Only one of the three survived. But not only rabbis acted in this manner; many simple Jews would refuse opportunities of escape because they would want to share the fate of all. For some time after their liberation many a survivor walked about with a guilty conscience for not having died with all his loved ones, with the rest of his people. As one of them, for instance, wrote: "I would like to do penance for the sin of survival, of having returned to life." [54]

The actions of all these people would have found little approval by the "informed" heart of a Professor Bettelheim. [55] Their actions were all "cowardly" in not being able to face the true nature of their situation and were holding on to values which had become useless in their predicament. The Sheftel family should have accepted their separation in order to make it more difficult for the Nazis to destroy them. Dr. Korczak acted "foolishly" in sacrificing his life to no purpose. The rabbis in Warsaw should have thought of their own escape, rather than sitting there like lame ducks waiting for the executioner. How uninformed a professor's heart may be about Jewish values and Jewish ability for self-sacrifice! For many a Jew there were more important values to be preserved and testified to than the mere preservation of existence. What is one to say of the tens of thousands of Jewish mothers who went with their children to the gas chambers rather than be spared by selection for "the other side!" All these are forms of heroism that a civilization that has spawned the kingdom of the ghettos and the death camps may not be able to appreciate.

3.

There are two motivations for the defamation of the martyrdom

of Israel during the Nazi-German phase of world history: a bad
gentile conscience and a bad Jewish conscience. The question
raised by the holocaust that concerns man most directly is not,
"Where was God?", but "Where was man?" The presence of God
in history or his absence from it is a complex theological problem;
the presence or absence of man as an ethical and moral agent is
a matter of experience. The Jewish experience in the ghettos and
the death camps made manifest in our days the collapse of man
as a moral being. There were, of course, exceptions; but especially
in Eastern Europe, acts of moral conscience in view of the great
catastrophe were few and far between. It was a Jewish catastrophe.
In terms of the spirit, however, it was a world catastrophe on the
widest possible scale. Apart from the six million Jews, the Western
claims that they represent an ethical civilization also perished in
the death camps and crematoria. Auschwitz ushered in the final
phase in the moral disintegration of Western civilization. It is not
pleasant to face the bitter truth. But if the victims themselves are
guilty of cowardice, of cooperating in their own destruction, then
perhaps the moral catastrophe of the West is less devastating. It
is a most ingenious way of finding a scapegoat. Unfortunately,
besmirching of the martyrs of the worst form of inhumanity will
be of little effect in the moral purification of the West. Either
something new will emerge from the ashes, or mankind is approaching its ultimate cataclysm. Auschwitz is like a final warning
to the human race.

Rather different is the case of the bad Jewish conscience.
There is little doubt that Auschwitz once again revealed the unique
position held by the people of Israel in history. As so often in the
past, the plight of the Jew became the point for the crystallization
of moral direction in history. That is the ultimate significance of
being the chosen people of God. As a Jew, one either accepts it or
rejects it. If a Jew rejects it, he has to abolish the character of
Jewish uniqueness. One is then obligated to "prove" that there is
really not much difference between the murderers and their victims.
The Jew, alienated from Judaism and historic Jewish destiny,
defames the martyrs of his people in order to find himself an emotionally more comfortable spot in the midst of a disintegrating West.

CHAPTER II

THE VANISHING WEST?

The disintegration of Western civilization, has produced two reactions which concern us in the context of our present discussion. The one is of a religio-political nature, the other is found in the realm of modern Protestant theology. In order to meet the tidal wave of dissolution, the Christian church has conceived the idea of ecumenism. As an answer to the collapse of the entire system of traditional beliefs, some of the younger Protestant theologians have presented us with what is known as Radical Theology. Both are, in our opinion, religious manifestations of the end of an era and a civilization. For the sake of Jewish self-understanding, it is important that Jews should evaluate both these manifestations of the universal crisis from the vantage point of their own unique experience. At the same time, in doing this they may render significant service in man's search for new directions at this hour of penultimate disorientation.

JUDAISM IN THE POST-CHRISTIAN ERA

Ecumenism has direct bearing on the Jew, since he has been invited to share in it in the name of a common religious heritage. What, however, the Jew cannot fail noting is the specific quality of the moment in history at which such an invitation has been extended to him. It is a moment when the Christian era is coming to its close.

The Christian era did not start with the birth of Jesus. It dates from the first half of the fourth century, commencing when Con-

stantine the Great established Christianity as the state religion of
the Roman Empire. The characteristic mark of the era was militancy. This was inherent in its beginnings: Christianity did not
capture the Roman Empire by the power of a religious idea but
by the sword of the emperor. As soon as Christianity was established, Judaism was declared an odious heretic sect whose propagation was forbidden under penalty of death. All other religions
were completely oppressed and actually exterminated. Christianity's
conquering march over all of Europe began. It was a conquest in
the true sense of the word: Europe was Christianized by the power
of the imperial sword. Before the Saxons, the Franks, and many
of the aboriginal tribes, was placed the choice: baptism or death.
Uncounted numbers chose death. *Cuius regio eius religio,* the
principle by which faith was determined in the religious wars that
tore Europe apart after the Reformation, was also the principle
by which, from the earliest days of the established church, Christianity was spread across the face of the earth. Even the vast missionary activities in Asia and Africa were possible only because
the Western colonizing powers which opened up these new lands
were Christian. The preachers of the gospel marched in the wake
of the swift and terrible sword of Constantine.

This era has come to an end in our days, before our own eyes.
It has reached its conclusion because the sword of Constantine has
been passed on to numerous other hands. The Soviets are holding
it mightily in their grip; Red China has taken possession of it; the
dark millions of Africa are acquiring it; hundreds of millions of
Moslems, Buddhists, and Hindus have learned to wield it. Christianity is no longer the decisive power or influence. From now on,
world history will be determined by the interplay of many forces,
many cultures and civilizations, most of them non-Christian, some
of them anti-Christian.

This change in the world situation carries with it weighty consequences for Christianity, which the Church, especially the Roman
Church, has not been slow to appreciate. *Nolens volens* the age
of Christian militancy is over; "baptism or death" is gone forever.
The reason, as we noted, is that now so many non-Christians, too,
have acquired the sword of Constantine. They can wield it no less
effectively than the Christian powers did in the past; they are in

the majority; and now they, in turn, have the power to
to oppress and persecute no less crushingly than did
through the long and dark centuries of the Christian

The new revolutionary distribution of the balance
the ecumene is ultimately responsible for the new C_____ ___
menism. An interesting illustration of this was provided by the
discussion on human freedom which took place at the Vatican
Council. It would seem that, notwithstanding the arguments in the
Council about the theological niceties of the final formula, the
Church now affirms the principle of freedom of religious worship
and human conscience. Following the discussion, we could not
help thinking of the old adage about the mills of God which,
though they grind slowly, grind exceedingly fine. We recalled that
freedom of religion and conscience existed in the Roman Empire
at the beginning of the rule of Constantine the Great. In fact,
they were affirmed anew in Constantine's own Edict of Tolerance.
But that was before he converted to Christianity. When Christianity
became the state religion of the empire tolerance was abolished,
freedom of religion proscribed, and freedom of conscience eradi-
cated. This state of affairs continued through the dark centuries
that followed in the form of oppression, persecution, autos-da-fe,
religious wars, and massacres. But now things are changing. After
sixteen centuries of Christianity regnant in the world, the Church
is ready to champion ideals that were already realized by mankind
by the time of the heathen Greek and Roman empires, not to
speak of Judaism and the secularisms of the last four centuries.
What has brought about this volte-face of the Church? Nothing
but the fact that Christianity is no longer supreme in the world.
When the Church leaders speak of freedom of religion, they mean
first of all freedom for Christians to adhere to their faith in Communist lands. When they affirm freedom of conscience, they mean
primarily freedom for the Church to propagate Christianity in
Asia and Africa among Moslems, Buddhists, Hindus, and among
the followers of all kinds of tribal cults. Christianity is now on the
side of tolerance because this is the post-Christian age of world
history, because in this post-Christian era the old policies of intolerance are no longer viable. Any policy of Christian intolerance
would be self-defeating for it would justify intolerance on the part

of the non-Christian powers, civilizations, and religions. It would ultimately boomerang onto the heads of hundreds of millions of Christians the world over. Ecumenism or no ecumenism, tolerance and a measure of official friendliness toward other religions and philosophies of life have today become matters of practical politics for the Church and for Christianity.

What should be the Jewish attitude, facing Christianity in the post-Christian era of world history?

We must, above all, understand history—that this is, in fact, the post-Christian era. We must understand the significance and the implications of this revolutionary change. From now on Christianity will have to rely for its propagation, as any decent religion should, on the methods of persuasion. All the friendlier statements about Jews and Judaism made in this new age by the Church and Christianity must be comprehended in the light of the change imposed by external historic developments upon Christianity. This certainly applies to the Vatican Council's schema on the Jews. It was forced on the Church by the new historic constellation. There are, of course, many Christians who feel ashamed of the abominable crimes committed by Christendom against Judaism and the Jewish people. However, the uncharitable haggling in the Council about the final version of the schema in itself proved that the sense of shame in some Christian consciences alone would never have sufficed to produce even that extremely guarded and political declaration.

An understanding of the implications of the new situation itself ought to help those Jews who are in contact with Church authorities and Christian leaders. Often they represent Judaism and the Jewish people without a mandate. At least let them speak with courage, self-assurance, and with all the dignity due to sixteen centuries of Jewish martyrdom in Christian lands. For the first time since the early days of the fourth century there may be a confrontation between Judaism and Christianity in freedom. Let it, indeed, take place in freedom!

Confrontation in freedom means that the scope of the confrontation must not be reduced to the provincial dimensions of Jewish-Christian understanding in the United States. Its significance must not be falsified for cheap considerations of public relations. Jewish-

Christian confrontation in freedom is confrontation in the world-historic context of Israel's own messianic history. In this new type of encounter with Christianity our generation must stand for all the generations that ever lived and suffered in Christian lands. It must stand for all the innumerable generations that never beheld the light of day because those who were destined to be their progenitors perished before their time under the bloody yoke of Christian oppression. We must face Christianity as the children of the *am olam,* the eternal people, viewing historical developments *sub specie aeternitatis.* I have never sensed so acutely that we are indeed the *am olam* as in these days when we are able to survey Christian performance from the beginning of the Christian era to its end. We have been there all the time; we alone know what it has meant.

It is our responsibility to sum up the meaning of that era, unimpressed by Christian claims, guided exclusively by our own experience. In terms of the Jewish experience in the lands of Christendom, the final result of that age is bankruptcy—the moral bankruptcy of Christian civilization and the spiritual bankruptcy of Christian religion. After nineteen centuries of Christianity, the extermination of six million Jews, among them one and a half million children, carried out in cold blood in the very heart of Christian Europe, encouraged by the criminal silence of virtually all Christendom including that of an infallible Holy Father in Rome, was the natural culmination of this bankruptcy. A straight line leads from the first act of oppression against the Jews and Judaism in the fourth century to the holocaust in the twentieth. In order to pacify the Christian conscience it is said that the Nazis were not Christians. But they were all the children of Christians. They were the fruit of nineteen centuries of Christianity—the logical fruit of violence and militancy, oppression and intolerance, hatred and persecution, which dominated European history for the sixteen centuries since Constantine the Great. Without the contempt and the hatred for the Jew planted by Christianity in the hearts of the multitude of its followers, Nazism's crime against the Jewish people could never have even been conceived, much less executed. What was started at the Council of Nicea was duly completed in the concentration camps and the crematoria. This has been a moral and spiritual collapse the like of which the world has never witnessed before for contemptibility and inhumanity. Judged in the light of our own experience and under the aspects of the messianic history of the *am olam,* we are confronting a morally and spiritually bankrupt civilization and religion. This knowledge should determine our attitude. In its light ought we define our position in relationship to the various issues which have arisen in the wake of this new Jewish-Christian encounter in freedom.

The schema on the Jews officially promulgated by the Vatican Council, has thought fit to declare solemnly before all the world that the Jews are not to be considered a people accursed by God; the Jews are not collectively guilty for the death of Jesus. We cannot help wondering whether, in the opinion of the leaders of the Church, these are still the Middle Ages or almost the Middle Ages. For many centuries, it was they who have been doing the prosecuting, they who perpetuated abominable acts of inhumanity against the Jewish people, but now they condescend to tell the world that we are perhaps not guilty nor to be considered accursed by God.

Underneath such lack of sensitivity to historical truth still lingers the barbarous concept that the fact that someone is persecuted and made to suffer by others is proof that something is wrong with him. For many centuries Christian clerics, theologians, and historians have maintained that the fact that Jews had lost their homeland, were scattered over the face of the earth, everywhere persecuted and held in contempt, was in itself proof that they were an accursed people, punished for the crime of having killed Jesus. In 1947 this thesis could still be found in history books written for the enlightenment of Christian youth.[1]

If it ever occurred to an isolated Christian that the "proof" was perhaps not altogether convincing, since it was man and not God who imposed all this suffering on the Jew, he could easily calm his conscience with the Christian logic of the Church Father, St. John Chrysostom, who showed that it was really God after all who was punishing the Jews. For, he argued, could man do all this to the Jews "unless it had been God's will?" By the same logic, not so long ago in Christian lands they would light the faggots under the poor creatures accused of witchcraft or cast them into deep water. If they burned or drowned, they were guilty of the crime of which they were accused. The Vatican Council's declaration about the Jews reveals how deeply rooted the logic of Chrysostom still is in the Christian psyche. Given the premises of Chrysostom's logic, it might seem Christian charity to declare that these Jews, though they suffered and were persecuted, are nevertheless not to be considered a people accursed by God.

This is, indeed, progress. A non-Christian, however, is not impressed. To such noble Christian sentiments he might prefer the teaching of the heathen Socrates, who maintained that it was better to suffer than to inflict suffering, nobler to be martyred than to inflict martyrdom. Followers of Socrates will be inclined to say that those who make others suffer are more likely to be a people accursed by God than those who are made to suffer by them. In this respect Jews are much closer to the heathen Socratic tradition than to the Christian. Many centuries ago their Pharisaic teachers interpreted for them the words of Ecclesiastes, "God seeketh that which is pursued," to mean: "The wicked pursues the righteous—God seeketh the pursued; the righteous pursues the righteous—God seeketh the pursued; the wicked pursues the wicked—God seeketh the pursued; and even when the righteous pursues the wicked, God seeketh the pursued." [2] Always God seeks the pursued. To be told after sixteen centuries of oppression and persecution in Christian lands by those responsible for these acts of inhumanity that the Jews are not a people accursed by God is an offense not so much to Jews as to God.

At one point, when it seemed that the Vatican Council was about to exonerate the Jewish people completely of the guilt of deicide, there were some precipitate Reform rabbis who felt that the Jews ought to reciprocate such a noble gesture by acknowledging Jesus as a prophet. It would seem to us that if there were to be any reciprocating Jewish acknowledgment, it should be commensurate with the Christian pronouncement. It might be said, for example, that the appropriate reciprocating gesture on the part of Jewry could be a solemn declaration that the man who endured the crucifixion is not to be regarded as accursed by God. Of course, Jews will never issue such a declaration, because they have never believed in Chrysostom's type of reasoning. Nor do they suffer from the iilusion that they personally and humanly represent God on earth. They are, therefore, in no position to dispense God's curse or His blessing. They deem it more respectful toward God to leave such dispensations to Him.

Many Christians and Jews are these days advocating the idea of a Jewish-Christian dialogue. The schema on the Jews recommends such "fraternal dialogues" in order to foster "a mutual knowledge and respect,." We ought to analyze this from several approaches— emotional, philosophical, theological, and practical.

We feel that, emotionally, we are not as yet ready to enter into a fraternal dialogue with a church, a religion, that has been responsible for so much suffering, and which is ultimately responsible for the murder of our fathers and mothers, brothers and sisters, in the present generation. There are, of course, Jews who are only too eager to undertake such a dialogue. They are either Jews without memories or Jews for whom Judaism is exclusively a matter of public relations, or confused or spineless Jews unable to appreciate the meaning of confrontation in full freedom. For Jewry as a whole, an honest fraternal dialogue with Christianity is at this state emotionally impossible. The majority of the Jewish people still mourn in a very personal sense. In a hundred years, perhaps, depending on Christian deeds toward Jews, we may be emotionally ready for the dialogue.

On the level of philosophical thought, contact and interchange of ideas are certainly to be desired. Jews are familiar with Barth and Tillich, Maritain and Gabriel, no less than with Sartre or Radhakrishnan. This, however, is not a specific Jewish-Christian dialogue. It is the dialogue in the intellectual realm which Judaism has carried on with all cultures and religions at all times. There is no more reason or need for a Jewish-Christian dialogue than for a Jewish-Moslem, Jewish-Hindu, Jewish-existentialist, or Jewish-atheist dialogue. The realm of thought is universal.

As to a dialogue in the purely theological sense, nothing could be less fruitful and more pointless. What is usually referred to as the Judeo-Christian tradition exists only in Christian or secularist fantasy. As far as Jews are concerned, Judaism is fully sufficient. There is nothing in Christianity for them. Whatever in Christian teaching is acceptable to them is borrowed from Judaism. Jews

do not have to turn to the New Testament for the "two laws";
Jesus was quoting them from the Hebrew Bible. And whatever is
not Jewish in Christianity is not acceptable to the Jew.

There are many who believe that Jews and Christians have at
least the "Old Testament" in common. This is a serious misunder-
standing. The Jews have no "Old Testament." The very fact that
for the Christians it is the "Old Testament" indicates that it is not
identical with the Hebrew Bible. This is not a matter of mere se-
mantics. The "Old Testament" asks for a New Testament; the
Hebrew Bible is complete within itself. The Christian interpretation
of Biblical Judaism is not the Judaism of the Hebrew Bible. The
Christian, reading his "Old Testament," discerns history and teaching which are essentially different from what is contained in the
Jewish Bible: from the Christian point of view Biblical Judaism,
as found in the "Old Testament" is altogether *preparatio evan-
gelica*—a preparation for the divine epiphany as the Christian
finds it in the New Testament. From the Jewish point of view,
the "Old Testament" is the gentile's misinterpretation of the very
gist of the message of the Hebrew Bible. When Christians use the
term "Judeo-Christian," "Judeo" means something fundamentally
different from what is Jewish for the Jew. Nor does Judaism have
a common spiritual patrimony with Christianity in the Patriarchs
and the Prophets: in Jewish understanding, the God of Abraham
is not the triune deity of Christianity.

There is a noteworthy contradiction as regards this matter of
the "fraternal dialogue" in the pronouncements of the Vatican
Council. On the one hand, the Council encourages dialogues with
other religions; on the other, it also affirms that the Roman Catholic
Church is the only repository of all true religion. What then is the
purpose of the dialogue for the Church? There is nothing that
Christianity may gain by it. The schema on non-Christians con-
cedes that other religions may contain some rays of divine light in
their beliefs and teaching. Yet, it is to be understood that all these
rays of light are comprehended in greater purity and perfection in
the Church. How then is dialogue possible? One does not enter into
a dialogue in honesty when one is convinced from the beginning
that one is in possession of all the truth and one's partner in the
dialogue is in error. This is not dialogical encounter. It can have

only one purpose—to spread the good tiding to the unfortunates who have not yet seen one's own light.

This, we have seen, is the post-Christian era. In former times Jews were commanded to appear before popes, bishops, and kings in order to defend their beliefs in religious disputations. These popes, bishops, and most Christian kings were also the judges. In these disputations the Jews could never be sure whether it was better for them to win or lose. It also used to be customary to impose on Jewish communities the indignity of compelling them to admit missionary preachers into the synagogues to listen to their sermons and boorish insults. These channels of "communication" with the Jewish people are no longer open. They are now to be replaced by "fraternal dialogue."

But there is no reason why Jews should be interested. It is not Judaism's ambition to save mankind, because it never maintained that mankind was lost without it. Judaism is the only possible way of life for Jews. Only Jews are lost without it. As to non-Jews, Judaism maintains that "the righteous of all the peoples have a share in the world-to-come." Judaism is free from missionary zeal. In turn, there is no reason on earth why it should make itself accessible to "fraternal dialogue" with a religion which, by its very premises, declares others to be in error and thus, from the outset, destroys the basis of a true dialogical situation.

But might not a Jewish-Christian dialogue have some beneficial, practical effects? Would it not further interreligious understanding? The strange reality, however, is that whereas among Christians it is the clerics, theologians, and the more committed and knowledgeable Christians who propagate the idea of interreligious understanding, the Jewish enthusiasts include the less committed Jews, the public-relations experts, the secularists. From such a dialogue, that in its very premises lacks intellectual honesty and emotional sincerity, it would be most unwise to expect any genuine deepening of interreligious understanding. The greater the hopes the greater the disappointments which must follow in such a "dialogue."

However, independently of all considerations of interreligious politics, we reject the idea of interreligious understanding on ethical grounds.

First of all, it represents a distortion of historic truth; it is a falsification of the true nature of the Judeo-Christian tragedy. It suggests a measure of mutuality in the responsibility for that tragedy; as if there had been friction and conflict because we did not know each other well enough; as if there had been struggle between Jews and Christians because they were not familiar wtih each other's noble religious traditions and beliefs. This is not the case. There were no conflicts or wars. There was only unilateral oppression and persecution. We reject the idea of interreligious understanding as immoral because it is an attempt to whitewash a criminal past.

Further, the idea of interreligious understanding is ethically objectionable because it makes respect for the other man dependent on whether I am able to appreciate his religion or his theology. In the official summary of the Vatican Council's schema on non-Christians we read that "the Council wants to foster and recommend a mutual knowledge and respect which is the fruit, above all, of Biblical and theological studies as well as of fraternal dialogues." We find repugnant the suggestions that mutual knowledge and respect among people should be the fruit of Biblical and theological studies, as well as of interreligious dialogue. It implies that if I am able to appreciate another man's religious beliefs I ought to respect and love him; if not, my contempt for him is understandable and justifiable. This is still conceived in the old questionable tradition of religious persecution. It is not a matter of whether Christianity acknowledges fragmentary truths in Judaism. All we want of Christians is that they keep their hands off us and our children! Human beings ought to treat each other with respect and hold each other dear independently of theological dialogues, Biblical studies, and independently of what they believe about each other's religion. I am free to reject any religion as humbug if that is what I think of it; but I am in duty bound to respect the dignity of every human being no matter what I may think of his religion. It is not interreligious understanding that mankind needs but interhuman understanding—an understanding based on our common humanity and wholly independent of any need for common religious beliefs and theological principles.

There are some who believe that, in an age such as ours, when religion is being assailed on all sides by secularism, materialism, and atheism, Judaism and Christianity ought to form a common religious front in defense of religious values and ideals.

It will be found that the policy of a common front may be laid down as a general principle only in areas of interhuman endeavor and not in the specifically interreligious realm. A common front is useful and necessary in the struggle for freedom of conscience and worship, for peace and social justice; our interests are identical in these fields of human striving. In the post-Christian era, how-ever, these goals of freedom, peace, and social justice have universal validity. It would be extremely foolish to seek their realization by means of a narrowly Jewish-Christian religious front. On the other hand, in the specifically religious realm, a common interest cannot be predicated as a general principle. There, Jewish and Christian interest may occasionally coincide in certain specific situations; in others, it may not. Under a condition of freedom, each group ought to decide on its course of action in accordance with its own insight and understanding.

The confrontation between religion and secularism occurs first in the intellectual realm, in the heart and mind of the believer himself. Here Judaism must maintain its complete independence. In the intellectual confrontation with secularism, Judaism must not become a mere adjunct to Protestant or Roman Catholic theology. Any close association with Christian thought is ultimately bound to cause confusion in Jewish thinking. It may cripple our ability to articulate the relevance of the specific Jewish position in our times. It would also be detrimental to Judaism's effectiveness: because of its fewer dogmas, Judaism is intellectually in a far better position to develop a philosophy or theology which can meet the intellectual onslaught of secularism. This is not easy, but it will be easier without the burden of a common religious front.

Even in the field of ethics and of the application of ethical principles to actual social or international conditions, one must be cautious about any joint Jewish-Christian endeavor. In many parts of Asia and Africa, Christianity has been compromised because of the close connection between colonial conquest and missionary activities. Closer to home, in the light of the Christian performance in the past and because of the practical requirements of Christian politics in the post-Christian era, it is not always easy to determine what is a humanitarian-ethical deed and what is Christian propaganda. An example to ponder is Pope Paul VI's peace mission to the United Nations. The speech on behalf of world peace was a fine oration. It came, of course, rather late in history. In earliest periods, a pope's stand on universal peace and brotherhood could have stopped wars, expulsions, and massacres. Unfortunately, when it could have been most effective—in the Christian era—the papacy was unaware of its universal mission for peace. Today peace is a popular slogan. What was once placed by Isaiah before the conscience of mankind as an ideal has now become an inescapable demand of practical world politics. Today the bomb itself is the most convincing argument for peace. "Make peace or perish" is its unmistakable message. In the final reckoning, when in a situation of world crisis the issue of war or peace in this atomic age will be decided, the pontifical plea will count for very little.

It would seem then that, on the whole, we have to go our own way. We have to work hard to make Judaism a significant philosophy of life in the intellectual climate of our age. We have to prove it to be a significant form of living which takes due cognizance of the moral predicaments of our days. We must equip it with the ability to articulate the truth of God in relationship to the vital issues of present-day human existence. If, as we develop our own position in the intellectual, ethical, theological, and religious realms of twentieth-century human endeavor, we find other religions working beside us, all the better. If not, we shall not be concerned. An awe-inspiring task lies ahead of us. Hard work, challenging and exacting, is to be done on the interpretation of Judaism and its implementation in this new era. We have every reason to continue with faith and confidence in our path. This is one of those rare turning points in history when we feel the breath of eternity about us. Having survived miraculously, the world-historic mystery of Israel has been deepened ever more by Israel's return to the land of its origins in accordance with the faith of the dark centuries of homelessness.

No one can foretell what this new era holds in store for mankind. But we are here at the threshold of the new age. We who were there when the Christian era began; we in whose martryrdom Christianity suffered its worst moral debacle; we in whose blood

the Christian era found its end—we are here as this new era opens.
And we shall be here when this new era reaches it's close—we, the
edim, God's own witnesses, the *am olam,* the eternal witnesses of
history.

THE DEATH OF A GOD

When a civilization dies, its God dies with it. The Radical Theology of Protestant theologians is an exclusively Christian concern.
It requires Jewish attention only indirectly. This Christian predicament may easily be misunderstood by being akin to the Jewish theological despair originated by Auschwitz. In truth, however, the
Christian problem arises from the very womb of Christian theology.
It is essentially linked to those aspects of Christianity which represent
Christianity's departure from Judaism. The theological disarray,
which is the true significance of Radical Theology, may well serve
as an added signpost by which the Jew may orientate himself the
better through a deeper insight into his own theological position.

1

"Radical theology," at the core of which stands the confession
that God is dead, is not all of one piece. One may discern different
trends and motives within this latest development of religious
thought, which its spokesmen insist upon calling a theology. We
shall limit ourselves to a discussion of four points which seem to
be the ever-recurring theme in all forms of this type of theology.
They concern man's new self-understanding, his new understanding
of the universe, his contemporary experience of the presence of
God, and finally, his awareness of the relationship between God
and man as it derives from modern man's God experience. As to
man, it is maintained, often not without a sense of pride, that he
has come of age, he has reached maturity. He accepts responsibility
for himself and the world. He is, therefore, no longer in need of
God. As to the universe, man's interpretation of its nature and
functioning is now purely scientific. Scientifically, the world is self-
explanatory. In our days, so it is affirmed, the universe has become
self-sufficient. It requires no transcendental reference for its

meaning. Objective knowledge has banished God from the cosmos. There is no longer any need for the idea of a Creator. Nor is it possible for modern man to have any experience of the presence of God. Since all knowledge is to be derived from experience, the realm of the transcendental itself has collapsed. All Absolutes have disintegrated. Man can know nothing of an Absolute Being. The very fact that the Wholly Other is wholly different from everything human places it outside every possible human knowledge. The only Absolute which is still recognized is absolute immanentism. Needless to say that on the basis of such a premise, there is no possibility for any form of God-man relationship. God has departed this earth. We know nothing of His presence. If anything, we experience His absence. It matters little whether He exists or not. In short, God is dead in our time and in our existence. With some "radical theologians" this development is the source of a new optimism. Now we may trust the world; we trust man, who has come of age. Others speak of the awesome autonomy that man is assuming now and see in it a tragic form of human existence.

It would seem to us that in the light of philosophical and theological scholarship all this is a rather meager fare. Neither the problems, nor the conclusions drawn from them, are in any way new. Original is the formulation of a not terribly original atheism as a theology. We have great sympathy with Van Buren's secular meaning of the Gospels, yet what he has done is apply the methodology of logical positivism and language analysis to the New Testament. Now, though logical positivism and language analysis have their value, they also have their limitations. The arguments pro and con are well known and we need not enter into their discussion here. It is rather naive to assume that the metaphysical problem of transcendence has now been philosophically resolved completely in favor of immanence. That the realm of transcendence has finally collapsed is treated by radical theologians as an axiom which requires no further elucidation. The idea appears in their writings more like a proclamation than a philosophical standpoint. But the matter cannot be decided by proclamation. To maintain that the scientific interpretation of the universe renders the idea of a Creator unnecessary shows no signs of either philosophical or theological sophistication. It may be so or it may not be so, but

one should not affirm it axiomatically, as is done by the radical
theologians, without ever entering into a significant discussion of
the philsophical or theological issues involved in the assertion.
Finally, that the absence of God, the lack of personal experience
of His presence means the death of God, be it the death of faith
in God or—as some would have it—God's death in a very real
sense as an event happening in time, is a most superficial way of
meeting the problem of the *deus absconditus* of metaphysics or of
the *El Mistater,* the hiding God of the prophets of Israel.

We believe that the "radical theology" is neither a theology nor
a philosophy. In its essence it is an attitude. Its thought content
is a rationalization of the attitude. This comes to clear expression
in a statement by Mircea Eliade, who has deeply influenced Thomas
J. J. Altizer, probably the most significant spokesman of "radical
theology." Eliade has the following to say on the subject:

> God has died as the result of an existential choice made by modern
> man. Modern man has chosen the realm of the profane; he assumed
> autonomy; he manages by himself; he has made himself a profane
> being.[3]

The rationalization of the existential choice into a "theology" is
not terribly interesting, but the reason for the choice certainly is.
It is of the utmost importance for Jews to understand what is happening in the God-is-dead camp of post-Christian theologians and
why it is happening. They call themselves Christian, even Christian
atheists, because the God they talk about and whose death concerns them is the God of Christianity. They are rightly to be known
as post-Christian. They all have in common the theme of the collapse of Christendom, of Christian teaching and civilization.

2

What surprises a Jew most is, I believe, the realization that for
the radical theologian modern man is God's competitor. God and
man face each other as enemies. It is either God or man. The
radical theologian does not only say that because of the scientific
interpretation of the universe there is no need for a Creator, but
he also adds that since man has no more need of God, he himself
becomes the creator.[4] It is not only that man has come of age and

accepts responsibility, but man may accept responsibility for his life, for the world, only now that God is dead.[5] Especially at this point the radical theologian leans heavily on Nietzsche and Camus. This relationship of competition to the death between God and man is again succinctly delineated in the words of Eliade when he says: "Man cannot be free until he kills the last God."[6] "Radical theology" implies—as its positive aspect—"the turning from the cloister to the world."[7] Strangely enough, only now that God has died in man's "existence" can man leave the cloister and turn to the world; only now, because he lost his God, can he live in the secular city in freedom and responsibility. We have mentioned earlier that some of the radical theologians speak of a new optimism of trusting man and the world. It is, however, noteworthy that for them optimism is a direct result of God's death. Thus, Hamilton, for instance, maintains: "I am persuaded that the death of God made this new optimism possible."[8] This competitive relationship between God and man is utterly foreign to the Jewish mentality. That the scientific interpretation of the universe requires no God hypothesis may be right or wrong; it has been held by numerous Jews. However, the idea that the throne vacated by God really belongs to Man the Creator, is clearly not a logical thought but one aspect of modern man's "existential choice" of a profane existence. It is a choice which, I dare say, is existentially alien even for an atheistic Jew. The causal nexus between God's death and human responsibility is equally foreign to the Jew. Within Judaism, from the very beginning, it was God who called man to responsibility and entrusted the earth into his responsible safe-keeping. Far from being able to "turn from the cloister to the world" as a result of God's death, it was God who never let the Jew turn to the cloister, but sent him into the world "to work it and to preserve it." We may understand that it is possible for a man to be optimistic about life and the world even without faith in God, but what kind of a distortion of the mind would require the death of God as the foundation of optimism? In Judaism, God is the only cause of optimism. For a Jew the strangest aspect of "radical theology" is that according to it, man feels crushed in his very being by God. In keeping with the Nietzschean exclamation, if there were gods how could I bear not to be a god, in "radical theology" man kills God in order to be able to choose himself in freedom and responsibility. What is the reason for this strange competitive relationship between God and man?

We believe that this "theology" could only have arisen in the midst of Christendom as an understandable reaction, long overdue, to some aspects of fundamental Christian teaching and dogma. Harvey Cox makes the penetrating comment about the philosophy of Camus that Camus knew that there was an essential contradiction between the traditional Christian doctrine of God and the full freedom and responsibility of man. And he adds: "A God who emasculates man's creativity and hamstrings his responsibility for his fellow man must be dethroned." [9] According to Cox such emasculation of man in Christianity is due to the absorption of Platonic and Aristotelian ideas about the idea of the Good as well as about God, which represented a fateful departure from the teachings of the Hebrew Bible. We believe that Cox does not go far enough in his analysis. The reason for man's emasculation by Christianity is much more fundamental; it goes to the very heart of Christianity. It is the direct outcome of the dogma of Original Sin. As the result of the Fall human nature became corrupt. Because of it, man can never save himself; he can do nothing good and worthwhile in this world; he cannot act with responsibility; he is completely subjugated by his fallen condition. He can only be saved by the miracle of divine intervention. The miracle occurred in the Incarnation. Because of it, and through his faith, man is reborn a new and pure being. But what happens if the act of redemption does not take place in fact; if, as a matter of historic experience, man is not renewed and the new Adam does not appear? Be the reason for it what it may, once the miracle of man's rebirth does not materialize, man remains degraded, robbed of his dignity as a human being. G. Vahanian is right in stating that "Christianity has often degraded, enslaved men, deprecated his creative imagination, the intrinsic worth of his finitude." [10]

However, in the teaching of the Fall, not only man became degraded but the whole of creation. Nature itself became corrupt, the entire universe fell into disarray; this world lost its value and meaning. Whereas man was to be redeemed, the earth was to be replaced by the Kingdom of God which was not of this world.

Christianity is an other-worldly religion. It has no use for this
world and no respect for it. But what happens when the Kingdom
promised does not come? The original Christian position called
for "the end of time" and "the end of the world." But ever since,
time has been going on and the world, this world, does not come
to an end. And man is left with an earth degraded, fallen, and
corrupt. Seen against the background of the Christian teaching
about the world, one may well understand, for example, Altizer's
insistence that the Christian concept of the Kingdom of God and
the dignity of the cosmos, as conceived by modern science, are
antithetical concepts. The affirmation of the one implies the necessary denial of the other.[11]

Vahanian sees, correctly, that a sound instinct led the founders
of Christianity to look for a speedy dissolution of the present world
order.[12] It was required by the intrinsic logic of the Christian idea
of redemption and the dogma of the incarnation. Jesus came and
went and, to use a Talmudic phrase: *Olam k'minhago noheg*, the
world continues according to its established rules as before. The
dissolution of the present world order did not happen. Ever since,
this world has remained a cause of embarrassment to the fundamental Christian position.

What we see today in "radical theology" is a rebellion among
Christians against a concept of God and redemption that indeed
treats man as a worthless creature, incapable of responsibility of his
own, as well as a radical rejection of the notion of a world that is
so fallen and so corrupt that its only hope is to be replaced by
another-worldly Kingdom of God.

3

Christianity is unable to cope with man who has come of age
by deciding to accept responsibility for managing his own life and
building "technopolis," the secular city. The problem has been
inherent in Christianity from its inception. The "secular city" is
olam hazeh, this world. The problem arises from what is known as
"the delayed Parousia." Jesus came and went, but the promises of
an other-worldly redemption remained unfulfilled. Yet, according
to the teaching, "the Kingdom" was at hand. It was to be revealed

by the second coming of the savior, which, according to the expectations of faith, was to be immediate. He never came again. What was to be done with this fallen, rejected, corrupt world, with the secular city of an unredeemed humanity? Troeltsch has aptly commented on the Christian embarrassment stating that, because of the delayed Parousia, Christianity had to adjust itself to some compromise between the demands cf an utopian other-worldly Kingdom and the actual conditions of human existence.[13] This process of compromising between unfulfilled promise and reality has been continuous, and it is possible to interpret the various phases in the development of Christian theology in its terms. In essence, at the very heart of Christianity there is a split between civilization and faith, between culture and redemption, between the city of man and the city of God. All Christian culture and civilization are the result of the compromise, a partial surrender of the originally sacred to the inescapably secular. The process of secularization, the death of God, started with the delayed Parousia.

Implied in the basic Christian position, in the Christian concept of redemption and the Kingdom of God, is a denial of history. Within Christianity there is no room for history. Mircea Eliade puts it this way:

. . . it must not be lost sight of that Christianity entered into History in order to abolish it: the greatest hope of the Christian is the second coming of Christ, which is to put an end to all History.[14]

Another author, quoted by Bultman, formulates the idea in the following manner:

To the Christian the advent of Christ was not an event in that temporal process which we mean by history today. It was an event in the history of salvation, in the realm of eternity, an eschatological moment in which rather this profane history of the world came to an end. And in an analogous way, history comes to an end in the religious experience of any Christian who is in Christ.[15]

That is nobly said. However, history does not come to an end. The overwhelming majority of Christians kept on living in history. They lived in society, got married, raised children, paid income tax, went to war, built cities, governed themselves and ruled the world. They were very much part and parcel of this world of time and quite removed from the realm of eternity. What was to be done about it? According to the compromise, salvation applies only to the individual soul, the inner man; the world, history, remains unredeemed. Bultman, for instance, distinguishes between universal history, to which Christianity cannot grant de jure recognition, and "personal history," consisting of the religious experiences of the inner man. As the Christian Kingdom and the cosmos are antithetical concepts, so also are the Christian teachings about redemption and history. Kierkegaard may define faith as absurd because it is, and must be, outside history. From the Christian point of view, all history is Fall and all culture falls into history. Modern man is choosing the realm of the secular because he lives in history and accepts it. Following in the footsteps of his master, Mircea Eliade, Altizer reveals one of the roots of his "radical theology" by saying: "We must have the courage to recognize that it is the Christian God who has enslaved man to the alienation of being and the guilt of history." [16] But the city is in history. If history is guilt and alienation, then the city of man is rooted in profanity. In order to shatter this concept of history so that he may be able to accept responsibility for his city, modern man has to desire the death of that God that does not let him be.

It is only now that we may analyze what may be called the basic issue involved in our discussion. Altizer refers to Dilthey and Troeltsch, according to whom historicism is a product of the decomposition of Christianity. To which he adds that historical consciousness is a product of modern man's choice of the profane. [17] Altizer may be confusing the cause with the effect; all-important for an understanding of "radical theology" is the equation between the historical and the profane. What is the meaning of the sacred and the profane that will yield such an equation? As has been shown in the researches of Eliade on the subject, in archaic religions, as well as in Hinduism, the profane and the sacred are dialectically related to each other. The definition of the profane contains the negation of the sacred, just as, included in the definition of the sacred is the exclusion of the profane. An either-or relationship prevails between them: either one lives in the realm of the altogether sacred or in that of the altogether profane. The sacred is the primordial Totality, it is the Real. Fall is separation from, as redemption is return to the original whole, submerging in the Real, the Sacred. There is no possibility here for a gradualness of transformation. One submerges oneself completely and becomes miraculously reborn, as if in a flash; what happens happens now, and now is eternity. In the salvation religions, the transformation in a now is the result of the mystical ritual. Altizer is anxious to distinguish between the backward-directed return of archaic religions and the forward-reference of Christian redemption. Be that as it may, the dialectical relationship between the profane and the sacred is also found within Christianity. The act of creation brought into being a perfect world, the primordial wholeness, the sacred. Because of the dialectical nature of the sacred, the Fall is of necessity a fall into complete profanity. The transformation of redemption is transfiguration; it is the miraculous death of the Old Adam and the birth of the new in a now. Redemption is not a process but an "event," the transposition from the realm of the profane into that of the sacred outside of time. In this context there is no possibility of gradualness of transformation, no room for the acknowledgment of history. History itself is the Fall. One must die to history and be reborn in the timeless miracle of salvation. Outside the miracle of salvation, outside of the kingdom of the sacred, there can be only profanity. Existence in history is of necessity existence without God, existence against God. This world, the city of man, is therefore not only secular, but profane. History equals profaneness.

Indeed, the Christian position confronts man with the choice: either the Kingdom of God or history; either divine redemption or human freedom and responsibility; either the city of God or the city of man. All along this line modern man has rejected the Christian position. He has embraced history, assumed freedom and responsibilty, and seeks the fulfillment of his life in the secular city. In terms of Christian teaching, he has chosen a profane existence. "Radical theology," seeking a way out of the dilemma, has dethroned the God that presented man with either-or choice between the "cloister" and the world.

4

Let us now attempt to define the Jewish position as it relates to the issues under discussion. The major difference between the Jewish and the Christian position with reference to our subject lies in the differing concepts of the sacred. Within Judaism the sacred and the profane are not dialectically related. One might say that within Judaism the sacred, as far as it may be a human concern at all,[18] is not found in the realm of Being, but in that of Becoming. The sacred *is* not, but has to be brought into being as the result of someone's action or behavior. The seventh day is not holy, but becomes holy when God sanctifies it. Israel is *made* holy by God and becomes holy by sanctifying itself. "Thou shalt be unto Me a kingdom of priests and a holy nation" is not a divine promise of other-worldly transfiguration and redemption, but a challenge to Israel, a task, a responsibility. Man is called upon to sanctify himself; to sanctify this earthly Adam in this world. *K'dusha,* holiness, is sanctification. And sanctification is a process in time and not a miracle outside of time. One is called upon to sanctify one's earthly life.

Creation within Judaism is, from the very beginning, the cosmos, as it is forever given to man to experience it and to understand it. Moreover, there has never been a cosmic disaster of the nature of a Fall into corruption and profaneness. The cosmos of biblical creation is not the "primordial Totality" of being, which, as the Real, is identical with the sacred. Since the sacred is the result of sanctification, the Real, in the primordial sense, is neither sacred nor profane, but amenable to both sanctification and profanation. From its very inception the cosmos is secular. However, in Judaism, the secular is not the profane, but the not-yet profaned and not-yet sanctified Real.

The idea may be found expressed in numerous variations in the Talmud and the Midrash. We shall let one quotation stand for many. At the conclusion of the story of the creation the Bible tells us that God saw everything that he had made and beheld it was *"tob m'od,"* very good. Rabbi Samuel, the son of Nahman, comments: "tob," good, that is the *yezer tob,* the good inclination in man; "tob m'od," very good, that is the *yezer ra,* the evil urge in him. How is this to be understood? How can one call man's inborn inclination for evil "very good"? is the question. And the explanation is offered: This means to teach you that were it not for "the evil inclination" man would not bother to build a house for himself; he would neither marry nor beget children; nor would he attend to the affairs of human existence. In other words the "evil urge" in man is the basic life drive within him. It is neither sacred nor profane. It is the reality of man's vitality; it is the original givenness of man's existence. It is the secular raw material out of which all human culture and civilization is to be shaped in the sight of God. It is there for man to be used for building houses, begetting children, building the city of man. But as one uses it, one is also called upon to sanctify it. At the conclusion of the creation, God looked around and saw his "secular" creation and believe it was "very good." That is all that man ought to know about it. The primordial real is the secular and the secular is very good because it alone is capable of being sanctified. In the primordial sacred there is no room for man. There all is whole, all is All. There if man wants to be, he must fall. But once he has fallen, he is doomed. He cannot help himself. He can only be saved from "without." Not so in the not-yet holy secular creation of Judaism. From the very beginning man has been placed into this world, not in order to die to it, so that he might be saved by the miracle of divine intervention for a Kingdom which is not of this world. He has been placed on earth that he may santify the secular, *l'taken olam b'malkut Shaddai*, and establish the city of man as the Kingdom of God. It is not either God or man. Man, according to his own strength, continues the work of creation and becomes, urged on by God's call, a humble associate of the Creator.

One may see the difference between the Christian and the Jewish approach reflected in a midrashic passage. The subject is couched in typical midrashic style in the form of a dialogue between God and Israel. Israel said to the Holy One, blessed be He: Thou knowest the hard power of the evil inclination! To which God replied: Remove ye it slowly, gradually in this world; and I shall remove it from you completely in the world to come. As it is written: "Cast up, cast up the highway, gather out the stones." And it also said: "Cast ye up, cast ye up, clear the way, take up the stumbling-block out of the way of My people. . . ." One may well say that the opening of the dialogue is the attempt to establish a position as valid which, indeed, is identical with the Christian stand. The suggestion is made that the evil in man is too strong for him. Man is helpless against it. He is a profane creature. Only God can save him. This is as far as Christianity got in the evaluation of the human condition. It is rejected by Judaism. A complete transformation of man may not be possible without divine salvation. But that can wait till "the world to come." In the meantime, there is a task for man in this world: the burdensome struggle of man with himself, the process of slow, gradual self-transformation.

Expressing it in philosophical terms, one ought to say that in Christianity the sacred and the profane are ontological categories; in Judaism they are axiological principles. Between ontological categories there is no possibility of gradual transformation. The profane must die in the transfiguration of the mystery of redemption; and the sacred must perish completely in the Fall. The profane is always altogether profane and the sacred is forever altogether sacred. As axiological principles the sacred and the profane are processes of becoming. The profane is never competely lost, for the secular, which has been profaned, is always capable of sanctification; the sacred is never perfect, for what has been sanctified may also be defiled. Redemption itself is a continuous process and is never final in this world. Sanctification proceeds by degrees; it is inseparable from the time process. This is implied in the words: "Remove ye it slowly, gradually." It is the stuff out of which history is made. It is the essence of the Jewish concept of history. The sacred is life's sanctification on earth. History is man's responsibility, it is one of the dimensions of sanctification. Here, within the God-given task of sanctification, is the source of man's freedom as well as of his responsibility. The God who calls man to responsibility is the guarantor of his freedom to act responsibly. As man accepts responsibility, he enters upon his God-given heritage of freedom. Or as the rabbis read it: "Freedom—on the Tablets." Granting him freedom and calling him to responsibility, God has expressed his confidence in his creature, man. This, notwithstanding man's disappointing performance in history, remains for the Jew the foundation of his optimism.

The concept of the Law in Judaism is closely linked to this aspect

of our subject. If the profane and the sacred are ontological categories, dialectically related to each other, then of course there is
no possibility for history. One is either damned or saved. That
is why the "Kingdom" has to abolish history. It is also quite logical
to say that the "Kingdom" also abolishes the Law. In the "Kingdom", in a state of salvation realized in eternity, there is no need
for the Law. This is authentic Jewish teaching. At "the end of
the days" the Law is fulfilled. Only man who lives in time needs
the Law; the redeemed soul, existing in an other-worldly kingdom
outside of history is in no need of it. However, once the Parousia
was delayed, once the compromise between the utopian other-
worldly Kingdom and the actual conditions of man's this-worldly
existence became necessary, once redemption had to be relegated
to the inner personal history of the Christian leaving universal
history untouched, the antinomian attitude of Christianity lost its
logic and validity. While in a Kingdom which brings all history
to an end, there is no need for the Law; outside such a Kingdom,
in the world of time in which man continues to live, man cannot
manage without law. Abolishing the Law of God there was itself
an act of profanation of human existence in time and history.

We have to point here to a rather naive aspect of "radical theology." In Christianity, faith in Jesus replaces the Law. As indicated, this has its own logic on the premise that the Kingdom is at
hand and this world is to come to an end. The premise, however, is
rejected by the radical theologian. On the contrary, the world, this
world is just about to come into its own. But what of Jesus? If
God is dead, he can no longer be looked upon as the Supreme Lord
who has descended from the Heavens.[19] All the Absolutes and all
transcendence has collapsed. Therefore, he was a man, but one
with a unique significance. On that significance "radical theology"
speaks rather vaguely and unconvincingly. He is said to have
liberated man from his old being and made him free for the future;
or else it is maintained that Jesus made man free for his fellow
man; or again, that he liberated man from the law. It is not quite
clear how, if God is dead, he could have accomplished any of
these functions, though he might be considered a noble human
being whose example may well deserve imitation. One of the
authors calls him "the standpoint alongside the neighbor."[20] For

Altizer, again, in keeping with his predilection for mystical opacity, Jesus represents "the Total Divine Humanity," [21] whatever that may mean. What we have here is rather old-fashioned humanism that would consider it a pity to let go of the historic figure of Jesus because of its humanitarian significance. These interpretations tend to confirm Feuerbach's thesis that God is a projection of man's ideal inspirations. God is the Ideal Man. Having lost God, the radical theologians hold on to the Divine Ideal Man. Only that in history ideals and noble intentions alone may not be a sufficient basis for optimism. Is freedom from the Law and from God alone enough guarantee that man will indeed take his place alongside his neighbor? Has man, indeed, come of age in our days, in which the air is still contaminated by the moral stench of the crematoria of Auschwitz and Treblinka? The Kingdom is to be built here in this earth. The Ideal Man is still only an ideal. Before he becomes reality, freedom will have to find its place in the context of the Law. Freedom and Law are the two foci of human existence in time and history.

5

Finally, we have to concern ourselves with the question of the absence of God, the problem of the *El Mistater,* the hiding God. For the radical theologian the absence of God means the death of God. Altizer discusses this aspect of our subject in the following terms:

God is not simply hidden from view, nor is he lurking in the depth of our unconscious or on the boundaries of our infinite space, nor will he appear on the next turn of an historical wheel. Totally committed as he is to the full epiphany of faith in the concrete moment before him, the contemporary Christian accepts the death of God as a final and irrevocable event. [22]

Here too, as so often, Altizer's meaning is somewhat obscure. As other passages in his writing show, Altizer believes that the Christian dogma of God's descent into the flesh represents the death of God as an event in history. At that moment, the transcendental God actually collapsed into immanent humanity. [23] Thus he perished. He is unique among the radical theologians with his interpreation. But they all have in common the inability to acknowledge the concept of a "hiding God," so important, for instance, in the theology of an Isaiah. We believe that this too is the result of their original Christian background. The "hiding God" can hardly be an authentic Christian idea. The entire purpose of the incarnation in Christianity is salvation, to lift man out of his profane existence and give him reality as a new being in the realm of eternity. This is the function of the savior, to be accomplished in the epiphany of the Christian faith. By its very nature it can be achieved by a God who reveals himself; by the visible breaking of the transcendental into the realm of the profane. The very nature of this God incarnate is divinity made manifest. This God cannot hide for he saves by his self-revelation. A Savior-God cannot not save. If he is in hiding, he does not save. If he does not save, he is not; his death is final and irrevocable.

The hiding God is present; though man is unaware of him, He is present in his hiddenness. Therefore, God can only hide in this world. But if this world were altogether and radically profane, there would be no place in it for Him to hide. He can only hide in history. Since history is man's responsibility, one would, in fact, expect him to hide, to be silent, while man is about his God-given task. Responsibility requires freedom, but God's convincing presence would undermine the freedom of human decision. God hides in human responsibility and human freedom. However, where there is no room for history, where redemption lies, not in a process of sanctification, but in the transfiguration of a profane existence into a new birth in eternity, there God cannot hide. He must be visible in the miracle of salvation; he saves by his epiphany. There is no room in Christianity for the hiding God. If he does not walk with me, if he does not talk to me, if he is absent, he is not, he is dead. This is the conclusion drawn correctly by the radical theologian from the absence of God.[24]

Christianity maintains that it has its roots in Judaism. But it has departed from Judaism in essentials. In the past, it could not do enough to denigrate the womb from which, according to its own confession, it has sprung. What we witness today in radical theology is a theological retreat all along the line along which Christianity departed from Judaism in order that, under Greco-pagan influence, it may become an other-worldly salvationist mystery religion. As a Jew, one notes with interest a trend in this new departure which, in the search for a way out of the predicament, is in fact a return to some of the teachings of the Hebrew Bible. The radical theologians have been greatly influenced by Bonhoeffer, who of course was not one of them. But, already, in the writings of Bonhoeffer the return to the Hebrew Bible is a strong tendency, especially in his preference of the prophetic concept of salvation in history to that of the New Testament's salvation of the soul in a condition of eternity.[25] Cox and Vahanian, both clearly influenced by Bonhoeffer, are the other writers in whom turning to the Hebrew Bible in search of solutions is strongest.[26] Whereas in the past, Christian theologians were wont to interpret the Hebrew Bible in the light of the teachings of the New Testament, we discern now a significant tendency to reinterpret the New Testament in the light of the Hebrew Bible. The old method of the Christian reading of the Hebrew Bible under the impact of the Gospels created the Old Testament of Christianity. One cannot help wondering what may be the eventual outcome of the new trend of reading the New Testament with the help of the Hebrew Bible.

6

Needless to say, the aspect of radical theology that comes closest to our specifically Jewish preoccupations is the problem of the absence of God. It is the problem of the post-Auschwitz generation. The *El Mistater,* the hiding God, is a Jewish concept; but the idea alone is far from being an answer to God's silence in the face of the agony of the concentration camps and the crematoria. Calling him the *El Mistater,* Isaiah says of God: "Verily Thou art a God that hidest Thyself, God of Israel, Saviour." In Christianity, because he is the savior, he cannot be a hiding God. But Isaiah calls the hiding God, Savior. We must know him even in his hiddenness. The *El Mistater,* in his very hiding, is Savior. Will our generation ever be able to behold in God's silence at Auschwitz the saving silence of the Redeemer of Israel? We are still far removed from an understanding of God's absence in our generation, in our history. And yet, what we make of his absence will ultimately determine the quality of our Judaism for generations to come, if not for all time.

In our search for the Redeemer in his very hiddenness, we shall have to weave into one great pattern of Jewish existence three decisive factors of our condition: the *hurban,* the destruction of European Jewry; the theological disarray within Christianity as revealed by radical theology; the rise of the state of Israel, the antithesis to the *hurban.* The moment in history at which we have almost lost our hold of this world completely, the moment at which the Jew had been almost completely eliminated from the City of Man, is also the moment at which the God of Christianity has come to grieve over the very same city from which he is being banished, as through the ages his followers were banishing the Jew. At this very moment in history, divine providence has placed into the hands of the Jew, in the form of the state of Israel, the secular city of man—for us to turn it into a City of God on this earth. Quite clearly, we have been called. How shall we, the post-Auschwitz generation, respond to the call of the—after all—not-so-silent God of Israel?

CHAPTER III

GOD AND THE HOLOCAUST

JOB'S BROTHER

For numerous Jews the Jewish fate in the ghettos and the death camps led to a crisis of religous faith. "Where was God all the time? How could He countenance the infliction of such suffering and degradation on helpless millions, among them untold numbers of innocent children?" The faith of many a Jew in the God of his fathers was choked in the smoke of the crematoria. And today, in the third decade after the last chimney was blown up in the German death factories, the questioning has not subsided. On the contrary, it seems to be on the increase. The Jews are gradually recovering from the quasi-paralysis of the imagination that at first took under its protecting wings the surviving remnant of their people. As they do so, the immeasurable extent of the tragedy may now slowly sink in without rendering them utterly incapable of confidence in a meaningful Jewish destiny. Thus, the quest for the place of God in that tragedy is gaining added impetus. Our concern here is with the authentic form of the quest. For there is also an inauthentic quest. It is the quest of those, who independently of any confrontation with the Jewish fate of our generation, have renounced faith in a personal providential God. They reject any faith in God or conceive God as an impersonal cosmic process that is by definition indifferent toward individual human existence. When they raise the question of God's silence at Auschwitz, it is done with the impure intention of proving how right they were all the time. We call it impure, because the quest is a mere pretense. One must approach the problem of faith presented by the crematoria in the agony of one's soul. He who approaches the problem cleverly, using it as proof, vulgarizes. Only the believer in the living God of Israel is involved in the crisis of faith of the death camps; only he can lose his faith on account of it. Undoubtedly, for our generation Auschwitz represents the supreme crisis of faith. It would be tantamount to a spiritual tragedy if it were otherwise. After the holocaust Israel's first religious responsibility is to "reason" with God and—if need be—to wrestle with Him.

The "reasoning" with God is a need of faith; it issues from the very heart of faith. When in Elie Wiesel's *Night,* at the hanging of the little boy, someone asks: "Where is God now?" it is the right question to be asked. Not to ask it would have been blasphemy. Faith cannot pass by such horror in silence. Faith, because it is trust in God, demands justice of God. It cannot countenance that God be involved in injustice and cruelty. And yet, for faith God is involved in everything under the sun. What faith is searching for is, if not to understand fully, at least to gain a hint of the nature of God's involvement. This questioning of God with the very power of faith stands out as a guidepost at the earliest beginnings of the Jewish way in history. Abraham wrestled with God over the fate of Sodom and Gomorrah. We note how the man, who in the humility of his piety sees himself as mere "dust and ashes" yet has the audacity to challenge God with the words: "The judge of all the earth shall not do justice?!" There is no contradiction here. The man of faith questions God because of his faith. It is the faith of Abraham in God that cannot tolerate injustice on the part of God. This is also the essence of Job's dilemma. The sustained fire of his plaint is not derived from his personal plight, but from the passion of his faith. There is no weakening of faith here. On the contrary. It is the very power of the faith that lends force to the accusation. What has happened to Job is wrong; it is terribly wrong because it is judged by the ideal of justice that Job formed for himself on the strength of his faith in God. That Job will not accept the arguments of his friends in defense of divine providence is not a matter of stubborn self-righteousness, nor is it due to a sense of exaggerated self-importance. What the friends attempt to do is to defend a wrong as justice. By doing so, they— without being aware of it—degrade Job's idea of God. Because of

his faith Job cannot accept a defense of God that implies an insult
to the dignity of the God in whom he believes.

The questioning of God's providence in the death camps was
taking place within the classical tradition of Judaism. Unfortunately,
unlike the case of Job, God remained silent to the very end of the   *yes.*
tragedy and the millions in the concentration camps were left alone
to shift for themselves in the midst of infinite despair. To this day,
theologians are arguing about the meaning of God's answer to
Job. Be that as it may, one thing is certain: in the denouement
God appears to Job; He makes himself known to him. Thus Job
is able to find peace with God in the words: "I had heard of Thee
by the hearing of the ear; / But now mine eye seeth Thee; / Where-
fore I abhor my words, and repent, / Seeing I am dust and ashes."[1]
No such denouement to the drama of faith took place in the
camps. To the very end God remained silent and in hiding. Millions
were looking for him—in vain. They had heard of Him by the
hearing of the ear, but what was granted to their eyes to behold
was "dust and ashes," into which they—and everything dear to
them—were turned. There were really two Jobs at Auschwitz:
the one who belatedly accepted the advice of Job's wife and turned
his back on God, and the other who kept his faith to the end, who
affirmed it at the very doors of the gas chambers, who was able to
walk to his death defiantly singing his *Ani Mamin—I Believe.*
If there were those whose faith was broken in the death camp, there
were others who never wavered. If God was not present for many,
He was not lost to many more. Those who rejected did so in authentic rebellion; those who affirmed and testified to the very end
did so in authentic faith. Neither the authenticity of rebellion nor
the authenticity of faith is available to those who are only Job's
brother. The outsider, the brother of the martyrs, enters on a confusing heritage. He inherits both the rebellion and the witness of
the martyrs: a rebellion not silenced by the witness; a witness not
made void by the rebellion. In our generation, Job's brother, if he
wishes to be true to his God-given heritage, "reasons" with God in
believing rebellion and rebellious belief. What is it then he may
hope for? He is not searching for an understanding, in terms of his
faith, of what had befallen his people. He is not attempting to steal

a glance at "the hand" of the Almighty in order to be able to appreciate what meaning the senseless destruction of European Israel might have in the divine scheme. To understand is to justify, to accept. That he will not do. He looks to his religious bearings. He desires to affirm, but not by behaving as if the holocaust had never happened. He knows that this generation must live and believe in the shadow of the holocaust. He must learn how this is to be done. If his faith is to remain meaningful, he must make room for the impenetrable darkness of the death camps within his faith. The darkness will remain, but in its "light" will he make his affirmations of faith, and it will accent his affirmations. The inexplicable will not be explained, yet it will become a positive influence in the formulation of that which is to be acknowledged. The sorrow will stay, but it will become blessed with the promise of another day for Israel to continue on its eternal course with a new dignity and a new self-assurance. Thus, perhaps in the awful misery of man will be revealed to us the awesome mystery of God. But when this happens, who can say that it will not be we who, seeking His consolation, in consoling Him shall find our comfort?

THE ABSURDITY OF EXISTENCE?

1

There is a simple way to resolve the crisis of faith presented by the Jewish death-camp experience. One may meet the problem with a resolutely negative approach and say that what happened was only possible because God has abandoned the Jew, because He is not concerned with what happens to man. One might cut the Gordian knot with the classical formula: "There is no justice and there is no judge!" This would be the Jewish version of what today has become known as radical theology. In its ultimate consequence, such a conclusion is a comprehensive statement about an essential quality of existence in general. What it says is that the universe is indifferent toward human destiny. Considerations of value are alien to the universal order which is impervious to questions of meaning. Anything that can happen may happen, for there is no one providentially concerned with the course of nature or history. Indeed, such or similar is the position of some existentialists. Camus, for instance, gave expression to such an attitude in his *Letters to a German Friend,* writing: "I know that heaven, which was indifferent to your horrible victories, will be equally indifferent to your just defeat. Even now I expect nothing from heaven."[3] This, we take it, is what is meant by the absurdity of existence. Life is absurd, it is without meaning. The only meanings, the only values, are those created by man. There is nothing beyond this existence, beyond this ethical indifference of the cosmos. There is no possibility for any reference to the transcendental for values and standards. Life is altogether man's responsibility, his choice and his decision; it is his fight against a meaningless fate. The meaning that man alone can create is the only justification for a meaningless universe. It is the most uncomfortable aspect of such a position that—if carried to its logical conclusion—it leads to a justification of nazism itself. If there is no possibility for a transcendental value reference, if existence as such is fundamentally meaningless and man alone is the creator of values, who is to determine what the values are going to be or what the man-made meaning is to be? Man, of course. But which man? Man as such, in the abstract, as a norm, does not exist. There is no Man; there are only men! There are only people; and they are of all kinds, with different temperaments, varied desires, and manifold self-created goals which set them at cross-purposes with each other. Camus spoke nobly when, after having declared his disbelief in an ultimate meaning of the world, he continued: "But, I know that something in it has a meaning and that is man, because he is the only creature to insist on having one. The world has at least the truth of man, and our task is to provide its justification against fate itself. And it has no justification but man. . . ."[4] These are beautiful words, but only because "the truth of man" here means the truth of the man Camus and that of other men like him; they are beautiful if one sympathizes with Camus' man-made meaning. There is no such thing as "the truth of man"; there are only "the truths of men." Himmler too was giving expression to his "truth of man" when at the close of the Final Solution he said to the assembled SS leadership: "To have gone through that, and to

have remained an honest man just the same, save for the exceptions due to human nature, that is what has made you tough and
strong. This is a glorious page in our history, never before, never
again to be written." ⁵ There is no hypocrisy here. The "honest man"
and "the glory" are genuine; they are the truth of the man Himmler.
Camus opted for the persecuted; Sartre, for an existentialism as a
form of humanism. But why should one not also be able to opt,
in the full honesty of one's self-made truth, for the idea of a master
race as the supreme man-created value? It is true that far greater
human suffering is likely to be found in a world in which the master-
race idea constitutes the meaning of life, but this is the complaint
of those who suffer. The infliction of suffering as such may well be
reconciled—as indeed it has often been—with the man-made values
and meanings of the persecutors. Some like to side with the persecuted; others enjoy cherry pie, while others again find meaning
in an otherwise absurd universe by feeding the crematoria with
human bodies. In a universe in which all values are based on
human choice and decision anything may become such a value.

What, on account of the Jewish experience at Auschwitz, attempts to emerge as a Jewish version of a death-of-God theology
has both an ironic and a tragic aspect. Its starting point is the
problem of faith raised by the German barbarism of the Nazi era.
In search of a solution to the problems, it arrives at a position
from which one may not only reject nazism, but, indeed, find a
"moral" validation for it as one of the man-created truths. This is
the bitterest irony. The tragic aspect of such a position we see in
the fact that it presents us with one of the truly great triumphs
of the Nazi German proposition. It is of the very essence of that
proposition that there is no personal God who is concerned with
justice, morality, or human suffering. Law and meaning are man-
made, and the man is the Führer of a teutonic master race. A negative response of the Jewish people to the Auschwitz experience,
the response of religious denial, affirms the first part of the Nazi
proposition, which is the premise to its teutonic conclusion. It is
indeed so. There is no personal God; no divine justice nor divine
providence, as proved by what happened to the Jews. It is tragic
because it is the true Hitlerian victory, the victory over Judaism
in the hearts and minds of Jews, by whose treatment Nazi Germany

too was going to prove God's indifference toward the plight of Israel.

If existence, as such, is absurd, it is vain to speak of man as the sole source of meaning. In an absurd universe, man too is absurd and so are all his self-made values and meanings. Camus himself felt this occasionally. One of the most lovable characters in his novel *The Plague* is Tarrou. In that important self-searching and self-revealing conversation that he has with the doctor, we are given the key to his personality. He is a modest man, he does not wish to be a maker of history. There is something lacking in his mental make-up, as he puts it; he cannot be a national murderer. All he understands is that there are pestilences on this earth and there are victims. And it is up to us, so far as possible, not to join forces with the pestilences. Of this he says: "I know it's true." But how does he know? Perhaps, he is on the side of the victims because of that lack in his mental make-up? It would seem, however, that Tarrou himself would like to know how he knows, how he could know with such certainty. For Tarrou, too, has a problem. What really interests him is how to be a saint. But since he does not believe in God, his problem is: Can one be a saint without God? "In fact [that's] the only problem I am up against today," he confesses. But is there a solution to the problem? One might say that nothing could be easier than its solution. Indeed one might fail to see a problem here at all. For without God anyone may be a saint within the terms of his truth. In Valhalla, Himmler's minions are "honest men." Of course, Camus' problem arises from the fact that for him to be a saint is defined in an exclusive manner, as being on the side of the victims and against the pestilence. But can one, without God, define sainthood thus exclusively? This indeed is a problem, an insoluble one. And Camus seems to have had some notion that there was no solution to his problem along the road he was walking. After Tarrou had unburdened himself of his self-revelation to Dr. Rieux, the two friends feel that they ought to do something. At this point, one cannot help being reminded of the haunting question in the aimlessness of *Waiting For Godot:* "And what shall we do now?" The two friends decide to go for a swim. For "really it's too damn silly living in and for the plague. Of

course a man should fight for the victims, but if he ceases caring
for anything outside that, what's the use of the fighting?" [6]

And so to prove to themselves that they do care for something
outside that, they go for a swim. At first this may seem rather
opaque, until we learn to understand the symbolic significance of
the swim. For in order to be able to swim, one has to leave the
town; one has to pass through the closely guarded gates of the
city of the plague; one must have special passes. Finally, far out
in the fresh water of the bay one is "at last free of the town and
the plague." The town with its pestilence is the symbol of the
absurdity of existence, and the fight for the victims is the meaning
introduced into this absurdity by man. It is the attempt to be a
saint without God. But it is not enough; it does not work. One has
to go for a swim in the bay, outside the gates of this absurdity. The
swim symbolizes the need for the beyond, for a transcendental value
reference. Without a sphere of reality where one is "free of the
town and the plague," existence is indeed too damn silly; without it,
why indeed should one fight for the victims!

2

We realize, of course, that one might say: It's indeed so. Without
that "swim" reality is damned silly. Yet, there is no Beyond to
which to go for the "swim," there is no possibility for any
transcendental reference. This has, to some extent, been the position
of logical positivism which denies the validity of all value judg-
ments and reduces all ethics to questions of merely subjective likes
and dislikes. Of course, the logical positivist is not an existentialist,
neither is he a radical theologian. He will not say that existence is
damned silly, because he is a much better logician than the existentialist. For if existence were indeed damned silly, no one within
its scope could be bright enough to notice it. If life were indeed
absurd, its absurdity could only be judged from a point that would
enable one to understand the distinction between the absurd and
the meaningful. But this point cannot be found within the absurd
itself; one would have to move beyond the realm of the absurd
and take that "swim" whose possibility is denied by the premise.
While the existentialist is not as logical as the logical positivist, he

certainly speaks more truly. For it is indeed so that, as we have heard Camus say, man has meaning because he insists on having one. Now this may not be very logical, but it is a fact, and facts enjoy the privilege of not having to conform to logic. Man's insistence on meaning is meaning. Even a nihilistic rejection of all meaning, including man's, is insistence on meaning and its affirmation. It presupposes certain standards of values by which existence is being judged. These values are acknowledged to be meaningful, but in their light existence is found wanting. As a result the original value concepts are rejected as mere illusions and the meaninglessness of everything proclaimed. Finally, a certain form of behavior is adopted as the only meaningful thing to do in view of all that absurdity. All the time man is in search of meaning. In the very denial of meaning, he affirms it. Man is meaning. But he is meaning in the universe. In a meaningless universe the denial of meaning would not only be illogical but impossible. Only because there is meaning in the universe can the question of its absurdity arise, not only logically but also existentially. If, then, man's insistence on meaning declares the world to have no ultimate meaning, what this means is that existence from a point of realized meaning makes demands upon itself for more meaning. Whether such demands are realizable is another matter. The nihilist declares that they are not. This, of course, he cannot prove, because such a statement is not provable. Nihilism is not a logical conclusion but a choice, an act of faith in the purposelessness of existence, a decision whose purpose it is to adjust ourselves to the fact that the meaning originally demanded of existence was found unrealized. But the adjustment is meaning and the original demand for meaning, whether realized or not, too, is meaning in the universe.

The idea of the absurdity of the universe may be entertained as a dogma to which a person may emotionally commit himself; it cannot be argued as a truth that takes sufficient cognizance of all of man's experience. At least, one would have to concede that there is enough reason in the universe to adjudge a great deal that is happening in it as absurd. Not only is there enough meaning to judge, but enough vital force to act for the realization of meaning. Camus never solved this problem of how one could be a saint without God, yet he—and many others like him—were such saints, struggling "against this universe in which children suffer and die." [7] But of course "the saint without God" is part of the same universe in which he finds the suffering children; and what is wrong with that universe because of the suffering of the innocent is right with it because of those who struggle against such a universe. In the very power of his rebellion Camus affirms this world, which he loathes. The extent of his rebellion against the evil which is life, is also the affirmation of the good, which is life, too. The problem of the good is no less serious a problem than the problem of evil. Anyone who, because of the problem of evil, concludes that existence is absurd has aggravated the problem of the good. He closed a gap and tore open an abyss.

KIDDUSH HASHEM—The Sanctification of the Divine Name

The universe cannot be dismissed that simply—and certainly not after the holocaust. It is true that nowhere on earth and never before in history could one experience the absurdity of existence as in the German death camps; but it is also true that nowhere else in this world and never before could one experience the nobility of existence as there and then. And the one is not unrelated to the other. At Auschwitz and Treblinka, in the camps and the ghettos, man sank to his lowest level yet, but there too he was exalted to his highest dignity. The story of man's degradation is well-known. Perhaps, in our sorrow over it, we have paid little attention to the greatness of man. Let a few examples stand here for what we mean by the experience of the nobility of existence even next door to the crematoria. One of the survivors of the Warsaw ghetto tells the story of how he and a woman were sought by the Gestapo. They were chased for weeks, living continually under the shadow of imminent death, changing their hiding place from day to day, until, finally they were trapped behind the accumulated garbage of a ghetto attic. The man was determined to sell his life dearly. As the policeman approached his corner, he jumped forward and got him by the throat. The policeman went limp in his hand, completely at his mercy. At this moment, "Sonya ran from her hiding place and shouted hysterically: Don't kill

him! Don't kill him!"[8] What manifestation of human dignity in
this Jewish woman, who after having been stalked by death for
weeks, becomes hysterical at the thought that her companion in
hiding should kill their pursuer! And the vaster the inhumanity that
surrounds her on all sides, the more awe-inspiring is the nobility
of existence that she exemplifies. At that moment there was no place
on earth holier than that dark and dusty corner in that attic in
the Warsaw ghetto. It was the Holy of Holies on earth, sharing
in the very majesty of Sinai, when God descending upon it, proclaimed His "Thou shalt not kill!" Who knows whether that
wretched little attic was not wrapt in even greater majesty than
Sinai! At Sinai God proclaimed, in the ghetto a hunted human
being, at the risk of her own life, enacted God's commandment.

The same witness tells us about his final escape from the clutches
of the SS, helped by fellow men, among whom an underworld
character in prewar Warsaw was most instrumental. Recalling his
feelings at the time when he finally was able to climb out from his
secret hiding place, he writes: ". . . I was a little dizzy and walked
unsteadily. But I felt a lifting of the spirit. In this dismal terror-
ridden life, three men out of the gray, frightened, brutalized mass
had shown humanity, tenderness, and friendly consideration. Under
no greater compulsion than a decent feeling of compassion they
had risked their lives for a fellow man."[9] Instances of this kind
could be multiplied without number. They occurred not only in
the less dehumanized conditions of the ghettos, but also in the
death camps. Another one of the survivors reports: ". . . I saw
death many times in the ghetto and in the concentration camps, I
looked into its eyes often. Yet always the way out would come
suddenly, as if by a miracle. Always a fellow-sufferer would appear
to help out in a dangerous situation, by giving a hand . . . once—I
shall never forget that— a friend risking his own life, brought me
a dose of antitetanus serum."[10] The cases of self-sacrificing humanity that have been testified to from the ghettos and the death
camps fill volumes. There is, for example, the farewell letter by a
member of the Jewish Council of the Warsaw ghetto to a young
woman who was his helper in his work for the starving children of
the ghetto and who, being a foreigner, was able to leave Poland.
The man had been rich before the war and, thanks to his inter-

national connections, could have easily escaped the ghetto and left Poland. He wrote to her: "I wish you a safe journey. I am not sorry that I remain here. Of all the decisions of a life which has not been a short one—I have just turned seventy—I consider the one to stay here among my brothers and sisters the wisest. And if my eyes shed but a single tear ... it was reward enough. Peace to you, my daughter."[11] When one day the last written messages from the ghettoes and the death camps will be assembled in an edition worthy of the depth of their truth and inspiration, mankind will possess in them a new collection of holy scriptures.

We have heard a great deal about the disgraceful behavior of some members of the Jewish police in the Warsaw ghetto and the inhumanity of the Kapos and of some of the ordinary inmates of the concentration camps. It is maintained that, occasionally, they were more cruel than even the Germans. However, before one makes such comparisons, one ought to look with greater objectivity at the conditions of those who are so judged. Anyone who is willing to take upon himself the trying responsibility of studying the records and documents of the conditions in the ghettos and the camps will soon realize that even in ghettos like Warsaw, life was so degrading and dehumanizing that it defies the imagination of anyone who did not actually himself share in the experience.[12] And the ghettos were sheer luxury compared to the concentration camps, of which a German official reported home that Dante's hell was a mere comedy compared to them.[13] The cruelty of the Germans surpasses everything known in the annals of human history. Yet, their greatest crime was not their cruelty, but their sophisticated system of planned destruction of the human status of their victims. Their terrible barbarous power over their helpless victims was not used just to destroy them physically, but to degrade them to the extent of losing the last vestige of their self-respect. The world has never known anything like that before. The cruelty of the Germans was different not only in degree from other forms of cruelty practiced by man against his fellow. Unique was their system of the planned dehumanization of their victims. It is the uniquely German crime against humanity, against the status of man. It is the crime most difficult to forgive or to forget. It has rightly been said that what the people had to face in the liquidation of the ghettos and on entering a concentration camp was immeasurable with all human experience and it defies all moral criteria.[14] Reading the reports and studying the documents, I personally cannot visualize how one could survive a single day in a German death camp. All the values of human existence were deliberately destroyed. Family ties were torn apart, not only physically, but morally, too. Parenthood was trampled underfoot. Compassion was derided. Whatever a human being ever cherished was degraded. And all this in conditions of ultimate physical misery and wretchedness. How could human beings endure it without losing their senses? How was it possible for them not to break down and lose the last vestiges of their humanity? A well-known type in the concentration camps was the "Moslem," the person who though, completely destroyed as a human being, went on living. Poliakov describes the "Moslems" in the following words: "When they could still walk they moved like automatons; once stopped, they were capable of no further movement. They fell prostrate on the ground; nothing mattered any more to them. Their bodies blocked the passageway. You could step right on them and they would not draw back their arms or legs an inch. No protest, no cry of pain came from their half-open mouth. And yet they were still alive . . . they had become insensible to everything."[15] Human beings can be crushed in spirit as well as in body. As there were physical "Moslems," so were there also moral "Moslems"—both the victims of German barbarism. The truth is that any act of cruelty committed by the victims of this inhumanly degrading system against their fellow sufferers was itself a German crime, the greatest of all their crimes, the crime of dehumanization. To compare members of the ghetto police or some of the Kapos to their German taskmaster is a sign of insensitivity for the monstrosity of the German crime against the metaphysical stauts of man. There is a universe of difference between the inhumanity of people who strut about as the lords of creation, battening on the fat of a raped and looted continent, who, in free choice, embrace a religion of cruelty and murder and use their terrible might for the systematic physical and moral destruction of helpless people, and the inhumanity of some of their wretched victims, whose innate humanity was pulverized under the crushing weight of the juggernaut of Nazi barbarism. The first

form of inhumanity is unnatural; the other, the collapse of the
human spirit under the maddening blows of unnatural cruelty,
natural—the natural and direct result of the unnatural. Inexplicable
is the fact that the overwhelming majority of the inmates did not
surrender their humanity to the very end; that, on the contrary,
there were not a few among them who attained to sublime heights
of self-sacrificial heroism and dignity of human compassion and
charity. This was the true mystery of the ghettos and the death
camps.

In former generations, at times of severe persecution, Jews
would affirm their faith through the supreme act of *Kiddush haShem*.
Placed before the choice of baptism or death, they would choose
death and thus sanctify His name. One of the tragic misunder-
standings of our generation is that people often imagine that during
the German-Nazi era in Europe, Jews were robbed even of this
opportunity of preserving their dignity through the sanctification
of the divine name. There was no choice. One could not opt out
of being a Jew. Nothing could be further from the truth. Choosing
death, when betrayal by baptism may secure life, is only one form
of *Kiddush haShem*, but not its only form. The classical example
of Jewish martyrology is the manner of the death of Rabbi Akiba.
As they were tearing the flesh from his body with iron-pronged
combs, "he took upon himself the yoke of the Kingdom of Heaven."
His disciples asked him: "Thus far?" His answer was: "All my
life I was worried by this verse—'Thou shalt love the Lord thy
God . . . with all thy soul . . .' With all your soul, it means: even
when He takes your soul. I said to myself: When will I have the
opportunity to fulfill it!" He prolonged the pronouncing of EHAD[16]
and surrendered his soul with the completion of the "Hear O
Israel." [17] When Rabbi Akiba was captured by the soldiers of
Hadrian, he had as little choice to die or not to die as the average
Jew in the death camps in Europe. He already had forfeited his
life. When his disciples asked him: "Thus far?" they did not mean
to suggest that their master save his life by renouncing Judaism.
It would not have helped him. He rebelled against Rome and was
under sentence of death. As the sentence was carried out Rabbi
Akiba was fulfilling a religious commandment: he recited the
Sh'ma, whose meaning is the acceptance of "the Yoke of the

Kingdom of Heaven"; the affirmation of one's love of God. The "Thus far?" of the disciple meant: Is one obligated to fulfill this commandment even at a moment of one's being forsaken by God? The question becomes even more poignant just because there was no choice before Rabbi Akiba. One might say that in the Middle Ages, when Jews were confronting the Church, their abandonment by God was not complete. The decision was still theirs; there was a way open to them, which they could choose and save their skins. As long as the decision still lies within man, a human being draws strength from his sense of self-respect. When it comes to matters of man's ultimate concern, strong personalities will rather die than save their lives by acknowledging a lie as the truth. This is not an exclusively religious act. Religious and secular people both have been capable of such martyrdom. The confrontation in such situations of choice is between man and man, man and society, man and some other earthly power. The defiant No with which a man meets a tyrant or a persecuting church or a humiliating falsehood is itself a supreme act of living self-affirmation. If it is done for the sake of God, in whose truth alone one finds self-fulfillment, it is a heroic act of *Kiddush haShem*. One dares speak only with great hesitation and trembling on the subject. It would, however, seem to us that with this act alone the highest form of *Kiddush haShem* is not yet reached. There is still a great deal in it for man. At this stage man is still acting within the frame of reference of this world. He preserves his dignity in the face of a this-worldly challenge. The ultimate phase of *Kiddush haShem* begins after the choice has been made. When the martyr ascends the faggots. The world has died to him, he is no longer of it. He confronts no longer man and his works. He is alone—with his God. And God is silent, and God is hiding his face. God has abandoned him. Now man is truly alone. If at this moment he is able to accept his radical abandonment by God as a gift from God that enables him to love his God with all his soul, "even when He takes his soul from you," he has achieved the highest form of *Kiddush haShem*. "Thus far?"—asked the disciples; "Thus far!"—answered the Master. Rabbi Akiba does not complain to his God asking why he has forsaken him. His radical abandonment is the great moment for which he has been waiting all his life. For no one can so completely surrender to Him as the one who is completely forsaken by Him.

The Jews in the camps never had the choice. They were placed directly into the situation at which their ancestors in the Middle Ages had arrived after they had made their decision. For them the challenge of *Kiddush haShem* commenced at the stake as the faggots were about to be set afire. From the very beginning they were beyond the gates of this world; from the very beginning they were facing God and not man. And God was absent; He had abandoned them. From the very beginning it was the *"sha'ah shenotel et nafshka,"* the hour in which He takes your soul. It was the classical situation of Rabbi Akiba. They did not choose it for themselves as did Rabbi Akiba or as was the case of myriads of instances during the Middle Ages. They were catapulted into it. But once in it, they were confronted with the ultimate phase of *Kiddush haShem,* to love Him with all one's soul at the very moment when He takes one's soul. For many the test was beyond them in strength; many doubted. Many exclaimed in their agony: My God, my God; Why hast thou forsaken us! But there were others, in the thousands and tens of thousands, who affirmed and acknowledged in the classical style of their Master, Rabbi Akiba, whose act of *Kiddush haShem* reached the ultimate of the love of God, because it occured in the dark hour of ultimate abandonment by God.

There is also another aspect of *Kiddush haShem* that should not be overlooked as we consider the human behavior in the ghettos and the death camps. The Talmud introduces the story of Rabbi Akiba's martyrdom with the words: "The hour when they took Rabbi Akiba to his death, was the time for the recitation of the *Sh'ma.*" In our opinion these laconic words hide the true greatness of Rabbi Akiba's deed. We usually imagine an act of *Kiddush haShem* as the stirring drama of the soul as it reacts to an extraordinary situation. This is how Jewish martyrs through the ages gave their lives and breathed their last with the words of the *Sh'ma* on their lips. It was an affirmation, an "acceptance of the Kingdom of Heaven," brought about by the extraordinary nature of the challenge; specific acceptance, meeting a specific hour. Not so in the case of Rabbi Akiba: it was the hour of the daily recita-

tion of the *Sh'ma*. Accepting "the yoke of the Kingdom," Rabbi
Akiba was doing what he had been doing every day of his life.
It was, one might say, routine. The extraordinary situation invested
the routine with extraordinary meaning and dignity. But Rabbi
Akiba was not responding to a situation; he ignored it. The Roman
soldiers came to fetch him; they abused his body. It happened to
be the time of the day when a Jew recites the *Sh'ma*. Let the
Romans do to him whatever they please; Rabbi Akiba could not
be concerned with it. He had more important things to which to
turn his attention—it was time for the saying of the *Sh'ma*. What
did it matter what Rome did to him! He went about his business
of living the daily life of a Jew. Continuing with "the routine" of
Jewish existence and ignoring the world that is bent on crushing
the Jew is one of the marks of *Kiddush haShem*. Often it is practiced long before the hour of radical abandonment arrives. *Kiddush
haShem* in this sense is not one final heroic act of affirmation. It
may be a form of behavior and daily conduct. Numberless are the
instances which show how widely this form of *Kiddush haShem*
was extant in the ghettos and in the death camps. Ringelblum, the
historian of the Warsaw ghetto, has the following two entries in
his journal. "I marvel at the pious Jews who sacrifice themselves
by wearing beards and the traditional frock coats. They are subjected to physical abuse. . . . An elderly Jew passed the guards on
Twarda Street and did not—for reasons of piety—take off his hat
in salute although the Jewish guards warned him. So they tortured
him a long time. An hour later, he acted the same way. 'They
can go to hell!' were his words." Now these Jews did not act
this way in fulfillment of any religious duties. From the point of
view of religious law, it was quite permissible for them to shave
their beards, to change their traditional garb. Nor was there for
them the least religious obligation not to remove their hats as they
were passing the German guards. Yet, they refused. And perhaps
one should not use that word. They continued in their Jewish
"routine," living their own life and ignoring the world around
them. They can go to hell! is a magnificent expression of this indifference to what the others are or do. One goes on being a Jew
in one's wonted everyday way. This too was *Kiddush haShem*. A
group of young Hasidim, their names are on record, are assembled

at the point whence they were to be taken to Treblinka. The cattle
trucks are not ready yet. There is time. It is Saturday at dusk,
the hour for the traditional *Sudah Shlishit* (the third Sabbath
meal). One of them finds some bread, some water. With the water
they wash their hands; they sit down to the Sabbath meal. They
intone the traditional song: "Let us prepare the repast of faith,
perfect and joyous, of the Holy King . . ." and as customary: "The
Lord is my Shepherd." [19] All this was done in the tradition of
Rabbi Akiba—contempt for a form of reality that does not even
deserve a reaction. The hour happened to be the time for the
Sudah Shlishit, just as Rabbi Akiba's hour chanced to be the time
for the saying of the *Sh'ma.* One is unimpressed by Nazi Germany
as one was unimpressed with Hadrian's Rome—one continues in
"the routine" of being a Jew. This, too, is *Kiddush haShem* and
it was practiced by many not only in the ghettos and at the assembly
points to the extermination camps, but also in the camps in the very
shadow of the gas chambers. Confronting Auschwitz one faces
ultimate evil, but also the ultimate of goodness. The vaster the
degradation and the misery, the more miraculous the manifestation
of man's faith in the values and meanings he cherishes. If the evil
was unnatural, so, too, was the good. Or shall we say super-natural?
If the humiliation was inhuman, so was the preservation of man's
dignity at all cost too inhuman. Shall we rather say, super-human?
It is our conviction that in our generation nowhere on this earth
have man's conscience and his faith in a transcendental meaning of
existence been defended and vindicated as nobly and as heroically
as in the ghettos and the concentration camps, in the very dominion
of their worst denial and degradation. Where we find man's deepest
fall, there also do we find his most sublime ascent. If man's ability
to perpetrate incomprehensible crimes against his fellow bespeak
the absence of God, the nonexistence of divine providence, what
shall we say of his equally incomprehensible ability for kindness,
for self-sacrificial heroism, for unquestioning faith and faithfulness?
Is this all man's doing? Is it possible to separate human nature
from the nature of the universe and from its meaning? Is it possible
to reject the universe and accept man? Is it possible to accept man
in view of his limitless ability for evil? Is it possible to reject him,

witnessing his equally limitless ability for good? These are, of
course, questions and not answers. But it is important to understand their relevance as we attempt to cope with the problematics
of existence as it emerges anew from our confrontation with the
holocaust. One must recognize the ambivalence which is inseparable from human destiny in the death camps. The ambivalence is
the source of the tragedy as well as the promise of existence. Meaninglessness recognized and fought is unrealized meaningfulness. It
is doubtful that any philosophy will ever penetrate the secret of this
ambivalence. It is, however, important that the faith by which a
man lives—and we all live by some faith—should take adequate
cognizance of its presence, woven as it is into the structure of
existence as it concerns and affects man. The question of faith for
the Jew is, therefore, not to explain why God was silent while the
crematoria were consuming a third of the Jewish people. The question is whether within the frame of reference of Judaism it is possible to take cognizance of the tragedy and promise of existence
and whether one may hold on to the promise in spite of the tragedy.
One of the survivors of Auschwitz—Birkenau, concluded her recol-
lections with the words: "I believe that the still small voice of Israel
will remain and continue to proclaim the law of truth and justice.
I have survived . . . now I know that fire cannot extinguish the
heart of man and gas cannot stop the breath of God." [20] It is not
our intention to justify God's ways with Israel. Our concern is with
the question of whether the affirmations of faith may be made
meaningfully notwithstanding God's terrible silence during the
holocaust.

CHAPTER IV

THE HISTORICAL CONTEXT OF THE HOLOCAUST

A JEWISH PHILOSOPHY OF HISTORY

We believe that the question has to be answered in the negative if we concentrate our questioning on the holocaust exclusively. We have to see the holocaust in the context in which it is set in contemporary history as well as in the sequence of the entire history of the Galut.

Chaos has engulfed the world. The very future of man is in jeopardy. The sickness is universal. We are aware of the dangers to human survival; but the new man who alone might be able to exorcize them is nowhere to be seen. It is difficult to hope and to trust—not only because the very air that we breathe today may choke us tomorrow, but mainly because the pollution within is much more serious than the pollution without, because the sickness of the human heart is by far more obdurate than the sickness of the human environment. It is in the midst of this chaos that the Jewish people has to look to its bearings, fully aware that its destiny cannot be separated from the destiny of the world community, that its own specific history is deeply involved in the history of the nations. Jewish history, like the history of no other single nation, has always been world history, for it has always reflected the moral history of mankind.

Never in the long history of the Jewish people has there lived a generation of Jews, having experienced so much degradation and humiliation as ours, that has also been granted such a rich measure of encouragement by the God of history as ours. The very same generation that has been compelled to drain "the cups of staggering"

to the last drop has also been handed "the cup of consolation."[1]
The survivors of Auschwitz and Treblinka recovered in Zion and
Jerusalem. They marched from the darkest pit of a man-made hell
into the light of Jewish sovereignty in the state of Israel—but not
to find peace there either. Universal chaos and pollution threatens
all men and, of course, the very existence of Israel. We who have
not yet been able to come to terms with the European holocaust of
our people, who have hardly had sufficient time to derive healing
comfort from the ingathering of the exiles in their ancient homeland, are once again confronted with the ultimate question of
Jewish survival. As far as the world's attitude to the Jew is concerned, the possibility of another Auschwitz cannot be ruled out
axiomatically. This world is quite capable of it. Those of us who
still remember the rise of nazism at the very heart of Europe, and
the benevolent international toleration which it enjoyed during the
crucial years of its consolidation, realize that the international
moral climate today is hardly more promising than it was prior to
the outbreak of the Second World War. The dangers are greater;
the fears and suspicions more pervasive. But how long can mutual
fear restrain the hand that holds so much power to destroy and is
guided by so little wisdom to heal and to build?

In order to meet the challenge to his very existence in the midst
of universal chaos and disintegration what the Jew needs most of
all is self-understanding. He must be able to appreciate the role
which he plays in world history and to acknowledge the principle
he represents in the human venture. He may then reject this role
and, thus, reject himself and disappear, or he may embrace it and
continue to strive and hope as never before. However, he can only
do that by placing the threefold experience of this generation—
Auschwitz, Jerusalem, and the new threat to Jewish survival—in
the comprehensive context of the world history of the Jewish
people, of Jewish teaching, and of Jewish experience. In the past
ten years or so, there were those who, mainly by way of literature,
have led us to witness, at least in imagination, the ghettos and the
camps, the gas chambers and the crematoria. There were also attempts to deal with the problems arising from the experience theologically and philosophically. The literature has been—in part—
disturbing, searching the depth of human nature and probing the

mysteries of the God-man relationship. It has compelled us to
make our vicarious pilgrimage to Auschwitz and Treblinka and to
open ourselves to the emotional and intellectual fury of their
problematics. The Auschwitz theology, on the other hand, has
been by far less fruitful. It has given us the rather naive radicalism
that eliminates God from history, or else it has led to a self-
imposed theological silence that refuses to interpret because it declares, quasi dogmatically, the absolute meaninglessness of the
holocaust. In our view, both the literary achievement and the
theological-philosophical attempts suffer from one serious short-
coming: they deal with the holocaust in isolation, as if there had
been nothing else in Jewish experience but this holocaust. The holocaust occurred after several millenia of Jewish history, and it cannot
be considered independently either of that experience or of the
teaching that accompanied the experience. Furthermore, the period
after the holocaust coincides with the rise of the state of Israel. But
neither must this event be seen in isolation. Standing by itself, the
state of Israel is a mere freak, a meaningless anachronism. Looked
upon as disconnected, apart from the rest of Jewish experience and
teaching, it is even less explicable than the holocaust. And,
finally, the renewed threat of another holocaust in Israel itself, and
the subsequent peril to Jewish survival all over the world, how is it
to be met in isolation by a generation that remembers only Auschwitz and has nothing more to hold on to but a few years of a
freakish independence? "Never again!" is of course the absolutely
necessary response to the European holocaust and to the threat of
a new genocide. But can a people, indeed, meet the challenge to its
very existence without a positive ethos of affirmation that may be
the source of its faith and hope? Can it be done with a desperate
"Never again" alone?

1

Is it possible to take cognizance of the European holocaust in
the light of Judaism's faith in a personal God? Can that faith
stand the strain placed on it by the catastrophe of our generation?
Raising such and similar questions we should realize that the problem of faith presented by the holocaust is not unique in the context

of the entirety of Jewish experience. In one respect the prospect of developing a positive approach in response to our problem is almost more frightening than the negative response of the ultimate meaninglessness of existence which we discussed earlier. Not for a single moment shall we entertain the idea that what happened to European Jewry was divine punishment for any sins committed by them. It was injustice absolute. It was injustice countenanced by God. But if we hold onto our faith in a personal God, such absolute injustice cannot be a mere mishap in the divine scheme of things. Somehow there must be room for it in the scheme, in which case the ultimate responsibility for this ultimate in evil must be God's. It is a frightening thought, yet one of the great prophets of Israel did not shy away from acknowledging ultimate divine responsibility for evil in the world. It was Isaiah who let God reveal himself in the words: "I am the Lord, and there is none else; I form the light, and create darkness; I make peace, and create evil; I am the Lord that doeth all these things." [2] Now the theological significance of such a statement is obvious. It is directed against Manichean dualism, which explains the universe as the work of two principles that are locked in continuous struggle with each other, the powers of light and darkness, of good and evil. The faith in the One God excludes such dualistic interpretation. But then, as Isaiah saw clearly, God as the only creator is also the creator of evil. How is it possible to adopt a meaningful attitude toward such a proposition? Following the neo-Platonic tradition, medieval Jewish philosophers maintained that evil was only a deprivation, the absence of goodness, as darkness is only the absence of light. [3] Quite clearly, this was not the opinion of Isaiah. It is needless to say that certainly after the holocaust such naive and well-meaning ideas have become more untenable than ever. The evil that created the ghettos and the death camps and ruled them with an iron fist was no mere absence of the good. It was real, potent, absolute. How, then, shall we understand Isaiah's declaration about God, who makes peace but also creates evil? What was Jewish teaching regarding it prior to Auschwitz?

The Jewish experience in the death camps of our times stands out as unique in the annals of man for the magnitude of the disaster, for unimaginable cruelty and unbridled inhumanity. Never-

theless, it is important to realize that the problem of faith presented
by the holocaust is not unique in the context of the entirety of
Jewish experience. From the point of view of the problem, we
have had innumerable Auschwitzes: There were the two destruc-
tions of the Temple of Jerusalem and the concommittant disper-
sions of Israel; there was the destruction of the great Spanish Jewry;
there were the massacres during the Crusades and the Black Death;
the Chmelnicki massacres and, nearer to our own days, the Petlura
pogroms. While the consequences of the second destruction of the
Temple have been more grievous than that of any of the other
tragedies, it is of course true that in the magnitude of human suffering and degradation nothing equals the tragedy of the German
death camps. Yet the problem of faith of the survivors of any of
those catastrophes was not different from the problem which confronts us in our days. The shock of those who perished in or lived
through the destruction of the Jewish commonwealth of antiquity
or the Crusades or the Chmelnicki period was not much different
from the experience of our generation. Surely there was no comfort for them in the fact that they had not known Auschwitz. Did
the Jews massacred in the Rhinelands in the eleventh and twelfth
centuries have less reason to ask where God was while those horrors
descended upon them than the Jews at Auschwitz and Treblinka?
Was the problem of faith in a personal God less serious during the
Black Death than it is today because then only half of the half-
million Jews of Europe perished and not six million as in our days?
While in absolute terms the horrors of the German death camps
by far surpassed anything that preceded it, in terms of subjective
experience the impact of the catastrophe on the major tragic occasions of Jewish history was no less intense than the impact of the
horrors of our own experience. The problem of God's providential
presence is always raised in relationship to man's subjective experience of His presence. The objective quantitative magnitude of
the tragedy has little to do with it. It is for this reason that while
the holocaust is unique in the objective magnitude of its inhumanity,
it is not unique as a problem of faith resulting from Jewish historical
experience. Indeed, one might say that the problem is as old as
Judaism itself.

But if so, before we may attempt to cope with our own contempo-

rary experience, we ought to recall how previous generations of
Jews have wrestled with theirs. As we try to understand the
present, we should familiarize ourselves with the manner the Jewish
people accepted and understood their destiny in the pre-holocaust
era of Jewish history, at moments of identical challenges to the
faith of the Jew. In order to come to terms with the hour of
history in which we find ourselves, we have to "remember the days
of old and consider the years of generation after generation." What
we need is a frame of reference for the world history of the Jewish
people within which the European *hurban* of Israel has to be
recognized.

2.

The problem of faith may be raised in a naive, simplistic manner,
for indeed there is the possibility for a naive and simplistic understanding of the Jewish frame of reference to history. When the
Bible says: "See I have set before thee this day, life and what is
good, and death and what is evil," this is a philosophy of life, which
at the same time represents a philosophy of history. And indeed
the Bible continues: ". . . in that I command thee this day to love
the Eternal Thy God, to walk in His ways, to keep His commandments and His statutes and His laws; that thou mayest live and
multiply, and the Eternal Thy God bless thee in the land whither
thou goest to take it into possession." But if you do not follow this
advice, "I have announced to you this day, that you will quickly be
ruined, ye will not prolong your days upon the land, . . ."[4] All this
is presented as a law of history. Your success or failure in history
depends on it. It was meant to be a philosophy of history that was
to be acted upon and was to guide the day to day policies of the
Jewish people, determining their decisions in any crisis or in the
face of any challenge. This is the consistent biblical message repeated on innumerable occasions by the prophets. God is a God
of history. He acts in history by destroying the sinners and causing
the righteous to prosper. One recalls, for instance, the mighty
words of Isaiah:

> Behold, the day of the Eternal cometh,
> Cruel, and full of wrath and fierce anger;
> To make the earth a desolation,
> And to destroy the sinners thereof out of it. . . .

> And I will visit upon the world their evil,
> And upon the wicked their iniquity;
> And I will cause the arrogancy of the proud to cease,
> And will lay low the haughtiness of the tyrants.[5]

This is what determines the course of history—a God who exercises providence and executes justice; and does this not only in the history of Israel, but also in the history of all nations. Such is history!

The idea was accepted with alacrity especially by Christian theologians. It was elaborated upon from Augustine in the fourth century to Bossuet in the seventeenth. This was to be expected. For the Christian mentality, the biblical suggestion explained pleasingly the misery of the Jewish people, as well as the remarkable this-worldly success of Christianity. It was good to know that those wicked, wicked Jews were punished, as they well deserved to be, for their stubborn rejection of the Christian claim in behalf of Jesus; and that the Christian faithful were duly rewarded with the empire of this world. All this made good Christian sense and it came from the mouths of the prophets themselves. Until, of course, that arch-heretic, Voltaire, appeared on the scene and tore this beautiful scheme of world history into shreds with his sarcasm and mockery. After all, the world was quite a bit larger than fallen Jerusalem and eternal Rome.

Voltaire was a viciously clever man, but in this case he had a comparatively easy task. Was the history of man indeed guided by divine providence, justice, and grace? Any child could see that it was hardly possible to reconcile the philosophy with the facts. Needless to say, Jews did not have to wait for Voltaire to disabuse them of a simplistic scheme of history that identified life with the moral good—or the good according to the faith—and death with evil. Already the prophets of Israel realized that it was not that simple after all. Jeremiah, for instance, cried out in his personal agony:

> Right wouldest thou be, O Eternal,
> Were I to contend with Thee,
> Yet will I reason with Thee:
> Wherefore doth the way of the wicked prosper?
> Wherefore are all they secure that deal very treacherously? [6]

If Jeremiah raised the problem of the success of evil in history, Habakkuk was baffled by the other aspect of the same problem, the suffering of the righteous.

> Thou that art of eyes too pure to behold evil,
> And that canst not look on mischief,
> Wherefore lookest Thou, when they deal treacherously,
> And holdest Thy peace, when the wicked swalloweth up
> The man that is more righteous than he? . . .[7]

Indeed, there is reason to contend with God. The facts do not fit the theory. This is, of course, the key theme of the Book of Job. If the theory is valid there ought to be no suffering of the just and innocent. Where is divine providence? As Job's friends attempt to resolve the dilemma, we are once again exposed to what, in the personal case of Job, becomes the heartlessness of the simplistic view; they turn to him:

> If thou set thy heart a right,
> And stretch out thy hands toward Him—
> If iniquity be in thy hand, put it far away,
> And let not unrighteousness dwell in thy tents—
> Surely then shalt thou lift up thy face without spot;
> Yea, thou shalt be steadfast and shalt not fear;
> For thou shalt forget thy misery; etc. etc. . . .[8]

However, as I see it, this was the last hopeless attempt in the Bible made on behalf of the simplistic theory of divine providence, justice, and grace. God himself—according to the text—rejects this defense of his world government. For after reconciling himself with Job, he spoke to Job's friend, Eliphaz the Temanite: "My wrath is kindled against thee, and against thy two friends; for ye have not spoken of Me the thing that is right, as My servant Job hath."[9] God rejects his would-be defenders and takes sides with the one who contended with him. Him he calls, "My servant," and not the friends who were bent on seeing in Job's suffering God's justice.

Far from disregarding the facts of history, the teachers of Israel in the Talmud were the first to speak of God's silence in history. In a discussion of the catastrophe of the destruction of the Temple of Jerusalem, they quote the verse from Psalms:[10] "Who is a mighty one, like unto Thee, O Eternal," attaching to it the midrashic comment of Abba Hanan, who explained it in the following manner: "Who is so mighty and strong (i.e., in self-control) as Thou, able to listen to the tormentings and insults of the evil man (Titus) and remain silent." There was the study house of Rabbi Yishmael, where they quoted another verse of the Bible:[11] "Who is like Thee! O Eternal, among the mighty" but replaced the Hebrew *Elim* by *Ilmim,* in order to make it read: Who is like Thee, O Eternal, among the silent ones![12] This is no longer a question, as the questions of Jeremiah, Habakkuk, and Job. It is not formulated as a problem; it is an exclamation: God, you are silent; you are not seen in history!

The Hiding of the Face

The problem thus raised by the prophets and the teachers of the Talmud is of course the age-old problem of the theodicy. The manner of its formulation testifies to the fact that there was a full realization in biblical and Talmudic times that there is indeed undeserved suffering in history.[13] This, of course, requires a modification of the concept of *Mipnei Hataeinu,* "Because of our sins." No doubt it does demand great strength of character of an individual—and how much more of an entire people—to acknowledge that one's misfortunes are due to one's own failings and to accept responsibility for them.[14] At the same time, looking at the entire course of Jewish history, the idea that all this has befallen us because of our sins is an utterly unwarranted exaggeration. There is suffering because of sins; but that all suffering is due to it is simply not true. The idea that the Jewish martyrology through the ages can be explained as divine judgment is obscene. Nor do we for a single moment entertain the thought that what happened to European Jewry in our generation was divine punishment for sins committed by them. It was injustice absolute; injustice countenanced by God.

In biblical terminology, we speak of *Hester Panim,* the Hiding of the Face, God's hiding of his countenance from the sufferer. Man seeks God in his tribulation but cannot find him. It is, however, seldom realized that "The Hiding of the Face" has two meanings in the Bible, which are in no way related to each other. It is generally assumed that the expression signifies divine judgment and punishment. We find it indicated, for instance, in Deuteronomy, 31: 17-18, in the words:

> Then My anger shall be kindled against them in that day, and I will forsake them, and I will hide My face from them, and they shall be devoured, and many evils and troubles shall come upon them; . . ., And I will surely hide My face in that day for all the evil which they shall have wrought, in that they are turned unto other gods.

But the Bible also speaks of the Hiding of the Face when human suffering results, not from divine judgment, but from the evil perpetrated by man. Even the innocent may feel himself forsaken because of the Hiding of the Face. A moving example of this form of *Hester Panim* is the Forty-Fourth Psalm, from which we have already quoted a short passage. One should study the entire psalm: we shall recall here only its closing verses:

> All this is come upon us; yet have we not forgotten Thee,
> Neither have we been false to Thy covenant.
> Our heart is not turned back,
> Neither have our steps declined from Thy path;
> Though Thou hast crushed us into a place of jackals,
> And covered us with the shadow of death.
> If we had forgotten the name of our God,
> Or spread forth our hands to a strange god;
> Would not God search this out?
> For he knoweth the secrets of the heart.
> Nay, but for Thy sake are we killed all the day;
> We are accounted as sheep for the slaughter.
>
> Awake, why sleepest Thou, O Lord?
> Arouse Thyself, cast not off for ever.
> Wherefore hidest Thou Thy face,
> And forgettest our affliction and our oppression?
> For our soul is bowed down to the dust;
> Our belly cleaveth to the earth.
> Arise for our help,
> And redeem us for Thy mercy's sake.

The Hiding of the Face about which the psalmist complains is altogether different from its meaning in Deuteronomy. There it is a manifestation of divine anger and judgment over the wicked; here it is indifference—God seems to be unconcernedly asleep during the tribulations inflicted by man on his fellow. Of the first kind of

Hester Panim one might say that it is due to *Mipnei Hataeinu,* that it is judgment because of sins committed, but not of the second kind. It is God hiding himself mysteriously from the cry of the innocent. It is the divine silence of which the rabbis spoke in the Talmud.

The Affirmation

Not only had the problem already been raised in all seriousness and full intellectual honesty in biblical and Talmudic times, it was also fully realized that at stake was God's presence in history. There was full awareness that the seriousness of the problem was apt to lead many a Jew to what is today called radical theology or the rejection of divine concern with human destiny. Ezekiel reported about the reaction of some people to the catastrophe of the destruction of the Temple and the loss of independence. He quotes their words: ". . . The Lord seeth us not, the Lord hath forsaken the land." [15] Like Ivan Karamazov, they too maintained that since God has absented himself, all was permissible. These were the early radical theologians in ancient Israel. The prophet Malachi, too, knew them. It is to them that he lets the words of God be addressed:

> Your words have been all too strong against Me,
> Saith the Lord.
> Yet ye say: "Wherein have we spoken against Thee?"
> Ye have said: "It is vain to serve God;
> And what profit is it that we have kept His charge,
> And that we have walked mournfully
> Because of the Lord of hosts?
> And now we call the proud happy;
> Yea, they that work wickedness are built up;
> Yea, they try God, and are delivered. [16]

"To walk mournfully because of the Lord" is not to walk like Ivan Karamazov, not to consider everything permissible, but to live obeying the laws of God. It is, however, useless to do so. God is not really concerned or, perhaps, he cannot do much about it anyway. For do not the wicked prosper and are not the proud happy? Is not evil successful? How may it be reconciled with God's providential presence?

Such were the radical theologians of old Israel. There is at least one outstanding figure known to us in talmudic times who belongs in the same category. He was Elisha ben Abuyah, at one time the teacher of the great Rabbi Meir. He lost his faith because he could find no solution to the problem of the theodicy. In view of the suffering of the innocent, he questioned God's justice and providence. He found no answer and became *Aher*, a changed person. According to one opinion he witnessed the accidental death of a young boy who was engaged in a work by which he was fulfilling a biblical commandment and also obeying the will of his father, thus honoring him as also required by the Bible. According to another version, he saw how the tongue of the martyred Hutspith, the Interpreter, was dragged along by a pig. He exclaimed at the sight: "The mouth from which issued wisdom like pearls should lick the dirt!" At that, "he went out and sinned." [17] There were others like him, less distinguished. Inevitably, in the course of Jewish history, the quest and the questioning continued. We even have a prayer for the radical theologian on record. According to one interpretation, in the abridged form of the *Amidah* we pray "For those who in this long exile are critical of God, believing that He has forsaken them. May they experience God's providential care, His mercy and grace." [1]

If Judaism rejected its radical theologians through the ages, it was not because of lack of sensitivity to the seriousness of the problem that they raised. The men of faith in Israel knew very well of the problem. They experienced it in their own lives on their own bodies. How often did they cry out in their agony over the terrible experience of God's absence! The Psalms, for example, are replete with the experience and the cry. Who could have felt the absence of God more crushingly than the man who exclaimed:

> Awake, why sleepest Thou, O Lord?
> Arouse Thyself, cast not off forever.
> Wherefore hidest Thou Thy face,
> And forgettest our affliction and our oppression?
> For our soul is bowed down to the dust;
> Our belly cleaveth unto the earth.
> Arise for our help,
> And redeem us for Thy mercy's sake! [19]

It was the excruciating experience of divine indifference that caused the psalmist to plead:

> How long, O Lord, wilt Thou forget me for ever?
> How long wilt Thou hide Thy face from me? [20]

The intensity of the experience comes to most moving expression in the phrase: "wilt Thou forget me for ever?" No one ever has an everlasting experience. The phrase tells of the long wait for divine help that was all in vain; it conveys the idea of utter hopelessness, of radical abandonment by God. The words would not have been inadequate for the agony of the death camps.

It is because of the apparent divine unconcern that the psalmist has to cry out:

> Arise, O Lord: O God, life up Thy hand;
> Forget not the humble.
> Wherefore doth the wicked contemn God,
> And say in his heart: "Thou wilt not require?" [21]

Such passages, and numerous others of the same kind, give expression to the struggles of men of faith against the demonic in history. They are the questioning, searching, yes! even the accusing cry of faith induced by God's silence in the face of evil. It is also the lament of Isaiah. when he declares:

> But Zion said: "The Lord hath forsaken me,
> And the Lord hath forgotten me." [22]

Obviously, to feel that one is forgotten by God is not a realization that one is being punished for one's sins. Whom God punishes is not forgotten by God. Zion's plight of being abandoned and forgotten is the experience of divine unconcern, of God's indifference toward human destiny. Through the ages, men of faith knew that human suffering was not to be explained by divine punishment alone, as expiation for guilt and divine justice done. They knew well that the poor and the weak were the victims, that wickedness and evil often held the upper hand, that God was often silent in history.

The experience of God's "absence" is not new: each generation had its Auschwitz problem. Neither is the negative response of resulting disbelief new in the history of Jewish spiritual struggle: each generation had its radical theology. Yet, the men of faith in Israel, each facing his own Auschwitz, in the midst of their radical abandonment by God, did not hesitate to reject the negative resolution of the problem. Notwithstanding the fact that so much in their experience tended to lead to the conclusion that there is "neither judgment nor a Judge," they insisted: "Still there is judgment and there is a Judge." Significantly, the formulation is Rabbi Akiba's, himself—as we saw—the saintly giant of Jewish martyrdom.[23]

However, if the problem was seen so clearly, how was it met? Needless to say, what we have called the simplistic theory of history that wishes to explain it all by the principle of "Because of our sins," the idea that if a man does the will of God and lives uprightly all will be well with him and that if he suffers his very suffering testifies against him, was indeed rejected. But the rabbis spoke of the silence of God as a historical fact, not of his absence. The one who is silent may be so called only because he is present. Somehow they are able to hold on to both ends of the dilemma. It is not an either-or proposition for them. Indeed the same may be said of the nature of the problem as it is originally raised in the Bible. The same Jeremiah who contends with God because the way of the wicked prosper, also refers to God as "the righteous judge who examines the reins and the heart."[24] He predicts the destruction of Jerusalem because of the sins of her people. Habakkuk, too, in the very same context in which he complains about God's standing by as the wicked swallows up the righteous also speaks of the scourge of the Chaldeans, "that bitter and impetuous nation" that is sent out by God "for a judgment and established for a correction."[25] In the same breath, he holds on to the theory of God's worldwide historic providence of justice as well as to the facts of history which seem to contradict it. This dramatic grasping at once both horns of the dilemma finds its most moving expression in Job, when he exclaims:

> Though he slay me, yet will I trust in Him;
> But I will argue my ways before Him.[26]

There is trust in God to the end; yet there is contest with him, because the facts of human experience seem to assail that trust. How was it possible for these men to retain their faith in the God of history, in his justice and providence, notwithstanding the fact that their own historical experience seemed to contradict the faith and the trust?

Much more astounding, however, is the fact that even though the Jewish people were fully aware of the conflict between history and teaching, yet they staked their very existence on the original biblical proposition that life and the moral good were identical, as were death and evil; on the view that all history was ultimately under divine control, that all depended on doing the will of God, on living in accordance with his Torah. Flying in the face of all historical experience, they organized their own existence in history on the proposition that "the Eternal is nigh unto all of them that call upon Him, to all that call upon Him in truth." [27] Nor did they do it naively, childishly, not realizing the full implication of their undertaking. After Jeremiah, Habakkuk, Job, and the divine silence actually experienced in their history, how could they affirm three times daily in their prayers that "the Eternal is good to all and His tender mercies are over all His works" [28] without a great deal of sophistication! A quality of this sophistication I find in a midrash that deals with our subject. It is a comment on the words of the psalmist, "The Eternal preserveth the faithful." [29] Playing on the Hebrew *emumin* (faithful) and its association *amen* (an exclamatory affirmation) and *emunah* (faith, trust), it is maintained in the typical midrashic style: "The faithful," these are those who answer with *Amen* in complete trust (*emunah*). What does this mean? They say: "Blessed be the One who quickens the dead." It has not yet come about, nevertheless they believe in God, that he does quicken the dead. They say: "Blessed be the Redeemer of Israel." But he has not redeemed them, except for a very short period, after which they became once more oppressed; yet, they believe that I shall redeem them. . . . O for the faithful whom God preserves. [30] One can almost see the sad smile on the faces of the rabbis who left us with this comment. "God preserves the faithful?" God the Redeemer, the Resurrector? Indeed? Yes, indeed. Nevertheless, and in spite of it all, it is so. We adorn God with a great many attributes which mean to describe his actions in history even though they are contradicted by the facts of history. Fully aware of the facts, with open eyes, we contradict our experience with our affirmations. Yes, all these attributes of God in history are true; for if they are not true now, they will yet be true.

The Explanation

1.

It would seem to us that what the just-quoted midrash wishes to convey is the idea that God is what Judaism believes him to be. True enough, many of His attributes are not manifest in history, but they will yet be revealed. On what grounds could such a statement have been made?

We have discussed earlier the two different forms of *Hester Pamin,* of the "Hiding of the Face": one as judgment, the other as apparent divine indifference toward the plight of man. We may glean a hint of the theological significance of such apparent divine indifference from a passage in Isaiah. The prophet says of God:

> Verily Thou art a God that hidest Thyself,
> O God of Israel, the Saviour.[31]

In this passage God's self-hiding is not a reaction to human behavior, when the Hiding of the Face represents God's turning away from man as a punishment. For Isaiah, God's self-hiding is an attribute of divine nature. Such is God. He is a God, who hides himself. Man may seek him and he will not be found; man may call to him and he may not answer. God's hiding his face in this case is not a response to man, but a quality of being assumed by God on his own initiative. But neither is it due to divine indifference toward the destiny of man. God's hiding himself is an attribute of the God of Israel, who is the Savior. In some mysterious way, the God who hides himself is the God who saves. Thus, Isaiah could also say:

And I will wait for the Lord that hideth His face from the house of Jacob and I will hope for Him.[32]

One may well wait and hope for the God who hides his face, if the God who hides himself is the Savior. But how may the Hiding of the Face assume this second meaning and become a divine attribute in such close association with God's self-revelation as the Savior? An analysis of a talmudic passage may lead us to an appreciation of this second—and more fundamental—meaning of the concept of the Hiding of the Face. It is no mere coincidence that it happens to be a discussion between Rabbi Meir and his quondam teacher Elisha ben Abuyah, who—as we have seen—became Aher, "another," because of the problem of evil on earth. It is said that after Aher had turned into the "path of licentiousness," he asked Rabbi Meir: "What is the meaning of the saying that 'God hath also made the one over against the other?' " [33] Answered the former disciple: "Whatever the Holy one, blessed be He, created in his world, he also created its opposite. He created mountains and he created hills; he created oceans and he created rivers." To which Aher countered: "Not like this spoke your master Rabbi Akiba. But said he: God created the righteous and he created the wicked; he created Gan Eden (Paradise) and he created Gehenna. . . ." [34]

The dating of the discussion as having taken place "after Aher had turned into the path of licentiousness" is an indication that the subject of the discussion has some bearing on Aher's problem and heresy. What is it they are discussing? It would seem to us that the subject of their discussion is the dialectical principle, which is seen as a principle of creation, incorporated in the functioning of the universe. Rabbi Meir expresses it in general terms. Whatever God created, he also created its opposite. It could not be otherwise. There could be no mountains without valleys. A thing is defined by its limits. It is recognizable for what it is by the contrast to its opposite. A is A because it is limited by non-A; it has selfhood because it is encumbered, because it is denied by non-A. Rabbi Akiba seems to express the same dialectical principle, but he gives it a limited ethical application. The dialectics of creation is responsible for the opposites: the righteous and the wicked, good and evil. Without good, no evil; without evil, no good! Why then did Aher oppose the general formula of the dialectical principle, holding on to the manner of its specifically ethical application by Rabbi Akiba? There is a vast distinction between Rabbi Meir's grasp of the dialectics of creation and the way Aher wants it to be understood. The example in the case, on which Aher insists, is adequate to illustrate the dialectics. However, it must have been noted that Rabbi Meir's example is somewhat gauche. The dialectical contrast would have to be between mountains and valleys, oceans and continents, not between mountains and hills nor between oceans and rivers. Yet, in his opening comment, Rabbi Meir invokes the dialectics of creation. It would seem to us that in Rabbi Meir's opinion the dialectics in creation does not represent pure opposites. The contrast is not absolute but relative. There is no absolute valley as there is no absolute mountain; the highest mountain is only a high hill and the lowest valley is really a bit of a hill. So too with the opposites of water and land. Neither the oceans nor the continents are absolutely alien to each other. The difference is only a relative one, like the one between oceans and rivers, like that between more and less. There is neither absolute depth to which to sink, nor absolute heights to which to rise. Aher cannot accept it, for the former disciple really discusses the problem and case of his sometime master. If the opposites of creation are absolutes, then good and evil too are absolutes; the creator is then directly responsible for both. He is then really beyond good and evil, for he is equally involved in both or, as one might also say, he is indifferent to ethical considerations. If so, Aher is right; there is neither judgment nor a Judge. It is for this reason that he insists on citing Rabbi Akiba whose formulation seems to suggest this kind of divine irresponsibility or indifference. The opposites, according to this version are the *Sadiq* (Righteous) and the *Rasha* (Wicked). God himself created both, is Aher's interpretation of Rabbi Akiba's statement. The *Sadiq* is what he is and the *Rasha* is what he is; the one is not to be praised, the other, not to be condemned. God himself created them that way. They are part of a universe that has no partiality for either of them. And once again, Aher himself is vindicated. It is exactly this kind of interpretation that Rabbi Meir wishes to obviate by his "bad" example of the dialectics. The opposites are not absolutes, which means they are not categories of creation. Rabbi Meir is not in disagreement with Rabbi Akiba. It is Aher who insists on an interpretation of Rabbi Akiba's statement that was never intended by its author. Rabbi Akiba never meant to say that God actually creates the *Sadiq* and the *Rasha,* that good and evil are indifferently incorporated in the universe. His whole life contradicts this kind of a teaching. Nor is it likely that Aher was unaware of it. It is with tongue in cheek

that he reminds his former disciple: "Not like this did your master
Rabbi Akiba explain it. . . ." Rabbi Meir spoke in general terms;
he did not expatiate on the dialectics of good and evil, of the
righteous and the wicked. Out of tact and consideration for the
feelings of his former teacher, he did not pursue the implications for
ethics and morality of a dialetics that does not recognize absolutes
as ontological categories of creation. Aher understood him well.
One imagines the impishly appreciative smile in his face as he
was saying: "Not like this did your master explain it. . . ." Indeed,
not like this; yet, exactly like this.

Rabbi Akiba expresses in ethical terms the significance of the
dialectics of Rabbi Meir. God does not determine in advance that
one person be a *Sadiq,* and another a *Rasha.* But unless the possibility existed for a man to be a *Rasha,* if he so desires, one could
not only be a *Rasha,* one could not be a *Sadiq* either. For one can
only be a *Sadiq* as a result of responsible choices made in the
freedom of available alternatives. Where the choice is nonexistent,
where the possibility of becoming a *Rasha* is not open to man,
the possibility of becoming a *Sadiq* too has been excluded. The
ethical significance of Rabbi Meir's "bad" dialectics is that being
a *Sadiq* is conditioned by man's freedom to choose the way of
wickedness, just as being a *Rasha* presupposes his freedom to turn
into the path of righteousness. The *Sadiq* is defined by the *Rasha*
as the *Rasha* is defined by the *Sadiq.* That which is good is so
because of the possibility of evil and vice versa. If, now, the
dialectical principle is at work in the universe yet the opposites
are not to be understood as absolute categories of creation and
being, then God's creating the *Sadiq* and the *Rasha* means that
God created both possibilities for man, to be a *Sadiq* or to be a
Rasha. We have quoted Isaiah's statement earlier that God forms
the light and creates darkness, makes peace and creates evil. Isaiah
of course did not mean to say that God actually does evil. Rejecting
Manichean dualism, the prophet maintains that God alone is the
Creator. He created evil by creating the possibility for evil; He
made peace by creating the possibility for it.[35] He had to create
the possibility for evil, if He was to create the possibility for its
opposite, peace, goodness, love.

In a sense, God can be neither good nor bad. In terms of his own nature He is incapable of evil. He is the only one who *is* goodness. But since, because of his very essence, he can do no evil, he can do no good either. God, being incapable of the un-ethical is not an ethical being. Goodness for him is neither an ideal, nor a value; it is existence, it is absolutely realized being. Justice, love, peace, mercy, are ideals for man only. They are values that may be realized by man alone. God is perfection. Yet because of his very perfection, he is lacking—as it were—one type of value; the one which is the result of striving for value. He is all light; on just that account, he is lacking the light that comes out of the darkness. One might also say that with man the good is axiology; with God, ontology. Man alone can strive and struggle for the good; God is Good. Man alone can create value; God is Value. But if man alone is the creator of values, one who strives for the realization of ideals, then he must have freedom of choice and freedom of decision. And his freedom must be respected by God himself. God cannot as a rule intervene whenever man's use of freedom displeases him. It is true, if he did so the perpetration of evil would be rendered impossible, but so would the possibility for good also disappear. Man can be frightened; but he cannot be bludgeoned into goodness. If God did not respect man's freedom to choose his course in personal responsibility, not only would the moral good and evil be abolished from the earth, but man himself would go with them. For freedom and responsibility are of the very essence of man. Without them man is not human. If there is to be man, he must be allowed to make his choices in freedom. If he has such freedom, he will use it. Using it, he will often use it wrongly; he will decide for the wrong alternative. As he does so, there will be suffering for the innocent.

The question therefore is not: Why is there undeserved suffering? But, why is there man? He who asks the question about injustice in history really asks: Why a world? Why creation? To under-stand this is of course far from being an answer to our problem. But to see a problem in its true dimension makes it easier for us to make peace with the circumstances from which it arises. It is not very profitable to argue with God as to why He created this world. He obviously decided to take his chance with man; he decided for this world. Given man, God himself could eliminate moral evil and the suffering caused by it only by eliminating man, by recalling the world of man into nothingness.

These theological concepts have found their more intimate expression in the language of religious affirmation. We are familiar with biblical passages that speak of God's mercy with the sinner. We readily appreciate pronouncements like the one in Ezekiel that declares:

> As I live, saith the Lord God, I have no pleasure in the death of the wicked, but that the wicked turn from his way and live. . . .[36]

In keeping with deep-rooted biblical tradition, the rabbis in a homily interpreted the plural form of the Hebrew expression that describes God as "long-suffering" as meaning that God is long-suffering in numerous ways. He is long-suffering with the wicked as well as with the righteous. We have great understanding for the fact that God is merciful and forgiving, that he does not judge man harshly and is willing to have patience with him. God is waiting for the sinner to find his way to him. This is how we like to see God. This is how we are only too glad to acknowledge him. But we never seem to realize that while God is long-suffering, the wicked are going about their dark business on earth and the result is ample suffering for the innocent. While God waits for the sinner to turn to him, there is oppression and persecution and violence among men. Yet, there seems to be no alternative. If man is to be, God must be long-suffering with him; he must suffer man. This is the inescapable paradox of divine providence. While God tolerates the sinner, he must abandon the victim; while he shows forebearance with the wicked, he must turn a deaf ear to the anguished cries of the violated. This is the ultimate tragedy of existence: God's very mercy and forebearance, his very love for man, necessitates the abandonment of some men to a fate that they may well experience as divine indifference to justice and human suffering. It is the tragic paradox of faith that God's direct concern for the wrongdoer should be directly responsible for so much pain and sorrow on earth.

We conclude then: he who demands justice of God must give up man; he who asks for God's love and mercy beyond justice must accept suffering.

One may call it the divine dilemma that God's *Erek Apayim,* his patiently waiting countenance to some is, of necessity, identical with his *Hester Panim,* his hiding of the countenace, to others. However, the dilemma does find a resolution in history. If man is to be, God himself must respect his freedom of decision. If, man is to act on his own responsibility, without being continually overawed by divine supremacy, God must absent himself from history. But man left to his freedom is capable of greatness in both—in creative goodness and destructive evil. Though man cannot be man without freedom, his performance in history gives little reassurance that he can survive in freedom. God took a risk with man and he cannot divest himself of responsibility for man. If man is not to perish at the hand of man, if the ultimate destiny of man is not to be left to the chance that man will never make the fatal decision, God must not withdraw his providence from his creation. He must be present in history. That man may be, God must absent himself; that man may not perish in the tragic absurdity of his own making, God must remain present. The God of history must be absent and present concurrently. He hides his presence. He is present without being indubitably manifest; he is absent without being hopelessly inaccessible. Thus, many find him even in his "absence"; many miss him even in his presence. Because of the necessity of his absence, there is the "Hiding of the Face" and suffering of the innocent; because of the necessity of his presence, evil will not ultimately triumph; because of it, there is hope for man.

MIGHTY AND AWESOME

In other words, God's presence in history must remain—mostly—unconvincing. But, perhaps, this is a mere theory, unsupported by experience? After all, how can one prove an unconvincing presence convincingly? There is another passage in the Talmud that leads us to a deeper grasp of our problem and its possible solution. Ezra, the great rejuvenator of Judaism at the time of the return from Babylon, and his associates in his endeavors were known as the "Men of the Great Assembly." The Talmud discusses the question of this honorific title. How did they deserve it? The answer is

given. They were so called because they restored the old glory
of the divine crown. The "crown" was described by Moses when he
called God: "the great God, the mighty and the awful." [37] But
Jeremiah, in the light of the experiences of his generation, could
not accept this description. He was perplexed. Strangers mock him
in his sanctuary! Where is his awesomeness? No longer did he
say of God, as did Moses, that he was "awful." Then came Daniel.
His charge was: Strangers subjugate his children! Where are his
mighty deeds? He stopped saying of God that he was mighty. But
then came Ezra and his assembly and they explained: "That
indeed is his mightiness that he subdues his inclination and grants
long-suffering to the wicked. And this in itself is a proof of his
awesomeness; for were it not for the fear of him, how could one
people (i.e., Israel) survive among the nations." [38] One might say
that as a challenge to faith the problems of Jeremiah and Daniel
were not different in essence from the problem of the present post-
Auschwitz generation of Jews. The vulgarity that God might have
died did not enter the mind of Jeremiah or a Daniel. But they
were perplexed by their God. How was he to be understood? What
were his attributes in view of the manner of his functioning in
history? If God's enemies feared him, they would not dare mock
him. If God were mighty, he would use his might to protect his
people.

Most noteworthy in this discussion of our problem is the complete antithesis in the position of the side that raises the question
and the one that offers the solution. The question as to God's
presence in history is raised on the assumption that the fear of
God ought to subdue the enemies of God and the power of God
ought to protect God's people. The answer is based on a radical
redefinition of the concepts of the fear and the might of God.
The mightiness of God is shown in his tolerance of the mocking
of his enemies; it is revealed in his long-suffering. This is in keeping
with the interpretation of the words of the psalmist that we quoted
earlier: "Who is like unto you among the mighty?"—enduring
insults and remaining silent. The awesomeness of God is revealed
in the survival of Israel. The meaning of the redefinition of the
concept of the divine power is twofold. First of all, it means that
it is impossible for God to be present in history by using his

physical omnipotence. If God had meant to rule the world of man by material might he might well have given up the thought at its very conception. Man can only exist because God renounces the use of his power on him. This, of course, means that God cannot be present in history through manifest material power. Such presence would destroy history. History is the arena for human responsibility and its product. When God intervenes in the affairs of men by physical might as, for instance, in the story of Exodus, we speak of a miracle. But the miracle is outside of history; in it history is at a standstill. However, beyond that we are introduced to a concept of divine mightiness that consists in self-restraint. For the omnipotent God to act powerfully would indeed be a small matter. The rabbis in the Talmud saw the mightiness of the Almighty in that he controls his inclination to judge and to punish and behaves in history as if he were powerless. To curb the use of power where infinite power is at hand, to endure the mocking of one's enemies when one could easily eliminate them, that is true strength. Such is the mightiness of God. God is mighty, for he shackles his omnipotence and becomes "powerless" so that history may be possible. In spite of his infinite power, he does not frighten man but lets him find his own way, extending to him his long-suffering. God is mighty in the renunciation of his might in order to bear with man.

Yet he is present in history. He reveals his presence in the survival of his people Israel. Therein lies his awesomeness. God renders himself powerless, as it were, through forebearance and long-suffering, yet he guides. How else could his powerless people have survived! He protects, without manifest power. Because of that, Israel could endure God's long silences without denying him. Because of the survival of Israel the prophets could question God's justice and yet believe in him. The theology of a God unconvincingly present in history alone might not have sufficed. The dilemma cannot be resolved on the intellectual level alone. And, indeed, neither Jeremiah, nor Habakkuk, nor even Job, were given an intellectually valid answer. The talmudic conclusion was correctly reached: God was silent. Yet, the dilemma was resolved, not in theory, but, strangely enough, in history itself. Now, historical facts that conflict with a philosophy of history *eo ipso* refute that philosophy. But historical facts, however numerous, cannot refute another historical fact however irregular and solitary. It is indeed true, as was seen by Jeremiah, Habakkuk, and others, that a great deal of the historical experience contradicts some essential Judaic propositions of a just and benevolent providence; the way of the wicked often succeeds, God is much too often silent. But it is even more true that seen in the light of the generally observed facts and processes of history, the very idea of a people of God, of constituting a people on the basis of a commitment to do the will of God and to the belief that life and death are determined by the ethical categories of good and evil, was a fantastic proposition. All history advised against it. From the very beginning, all the powers and processes that determine the course of history were poised to render its materialization impossible. Indeed, had it all been only an idea, a theology or philosophy, the testimony of the facts of history would have rendered the concept of a people of God and the propositions on which it was to be based ridiculously absurd. However, this fantastic concept became itself a fact of history. The people of God did come into being; it entered history, it became itself a historical reality, exercising great historical influence and demonstrating mysterious survival power. It has all been quite irregular. It is all in conflict with the rest of historical experience, yet itself a fact of history.

There is this difference between a fact and an idea. The more irregular an idea is, i.e., the less it is in harmony with the generally prevailing principles relevant to it, the less the likelihood that it is valid and true. The same may be said of a philosophy of history: the more it is contradicted by historical experience, the less tenable it is. But a fact obeys the opposite rule. The more irregular it is, the more unique it is, the less in keeping with what is generally observed and experienced, the greater is its significance. The more intensely a unique historical reality is disavowed and challenged by the overwhelming force of a universal historical experience, and yet it is able to maintain itself and to survive all conflicts and all challenges, has by its very staying power proved its unique vitality as well as the validity of the principle which it proclaims. Such a unique and absurdly irregular historic fact has been the people of God. But because it is a historic fact of inexplicable surviving power, the more it is challenged by the facts of universal history, the more is it confirmed in the unique stands which it takes, simply because it does take that stand and survives in spite of it all. Jeremiah could face with complete intellectual honesty the unpleasant fact that the way of the wicked does prosper, without embracing it as an ultimate truth in history upon which to base a Machiavellian type of philosophy. He could do that because the reality of Israel, notwithstanding all its contemporary misery, pointed as a fact in the opposite direction. The rabbis of the Talmud could speak of the silence of God at the time of the destruction of the Temple and the state and yet remain true to His word, because notwithstanding the *hurban* Israel survived, remained historically viable, full of future expectation.

This, however, means that a Jewish philosophy of history is not to be based on the teachings alone. The teaching, as such, is contradicted by a great deal of historical experience. But neither should Jews allow such conflicting evidence to sway them in determining their outlook on history, for such evidence itself is contradicted by their own existence, by the historic reality of Israel, by the place of the Jewish people in history, by the survival of the people of God; yes, by the fact that once again this people of God is back in its ancient homeland, in Zion and Jerusalem.

It would seem to us that there are two histories: one, that of the nations and the other, that of Israel. The history of the nations is self-explanatory. It is naturalistic history, explainable in terms of power and economics. It is exactly on those terms that the history of Israel remains a sealed secret: it defies that kind of interpretation. The history of Israel alone is not self-explanatory; it testifies to a supra-natural dimension jutting into history. Now, if the two could have been neatly divided and separated from each other, things might have worked out quite nicely. There would not have been either antisemitism or pogroms, either ghettos or crematoria. But unavoidably, both histories take place in the same time dimension and occupy the same space; together they form the history of mankind. Of necessity, the two histories interpenetrate. Thus, in the naturalistic realm occasionally the Voice is heard and a glimpse is gained of the presence of the supra-natural in this world. On the other hand, the wild unbridled forces of the naturalistic realm ever so often invade—and wreak havoc in—the this-worldly domain in which sustenance of meaning and purpose is drawn from the super-natural dimension.

Jews are confused in our times because they imagine that the problem of Jewish faith arises from the conflict between Jewish teaching and Jewish or general historical experience. In fact, the conflict takes place between two histories. There are two realms: the realm of the Is and that of the Ought. The history of the nations is enacted mainly in the realm of the Is. It is naturalistic history, essentially power history. The history of Israel belongs chiefly into the realm of the Ought; it is faith history, faith that what ought to be, what ought to determine and guide human life, should be and will be. Faith history is at cross-purposes with power history, but history it is. As long as Israel lives the Ought holds on to reality be it only by the skin of its teeth. As long as this is the case, the Ought has proved its vitality as a this-worldly possibility; it has found admittance into the realm of the Is. As long as Israel is, the Ought to, is; the Supernatural has acquired a footing in the Natural. As long as this is so there is hope for both—for there is hope for the ultimate merger of the two realms, when the Ought will be fully real and the real will be convincingly identified as the life which is the Good. In the meantime the conflict obtains, not between ideas and philosophies, which is easily bearable, but between fact and fact; between the powerful reality of the Is and the meaningful and mysterious reality of the Ought. Since it is a conflict between fact and fact, history and history, reality and reality, the conflict is clash, a battle accompanied by untold human suffering.

Why has it been so arranged by the God of history? We may not find an explanation. Decisive is, however, the realization that no matter what our solution may be to our specific problems, it must not abandon the truth to which the reality of Israel testifies. No matter how silent God may every so often be, we have heard his voice and because of that we know his word; no matter how empty of God vast tracts of the waste lands of history may appear to be, we know of his presence as we stand astounded contemplating our own existence. True, these are contradictory experiences which present the mind with a serious dilemma. But no matter how serious the dilemma, it cannot erase the fact of the enduring reality of Israel. Even if no answers could be found we would still be left with the only alternative with which Job too was left, i.e., of contending with God while trusting in him, of questioning while believing, inquiring with our minds yet knowing in our hearts! And even as we search for the answer, praising Him as the rabbis of old did: who is like you our God, mighty in silence!

CHAPTER V

THE WITNESS

God's unconvincing presence in history is testified to through the survival of Israel. All God's miracles occur outside of history. When God acts with manifest power, history is at a standstill. The only exception to the rule is the historic reality of Israel. That faith history has not been erased from the face of the earth by power history, notwithstanding the incalculable material superiority of the forces arrayed against it all through history, is the ultimate miracle. Since, however, it has been accomplished without manifest divine intervention, it remains within history, the only miracle that is a historic event, the miracle of the viability of faith history. It is for this reason that Isaiah coud say of Israel on behalf of God: "Therefore ye are My witnesses, saith the Eternal, and I am God." [1] Rightly do the rabbis add the comment: If you are my witnesses, I am God; if you do not witness, I am—as it were— no God. There is no other witness that God is present in history but the history of the Jewish people. God's own destiny in history is joined to the history of Israel. Great empires do not testify to divine presence in history. Whatever they are and accomplish is fully explicable in terms of their material resources. They have their self-explanatory place in power history. Half a billion Christians all over the world prove nothing about God's presence in history. They are too many, too influential, too pervasive. They are a this-worldly power in the context of power history. The same is true of any other of the great world religions. They have too many followers, control too much territory, too many resources of influence and power to prove anything. God is a mere adjunct to their position in history. Their religious affirmatives are incidental to their position in history. They all function in power history. Only a small people whose very existence is forever assailed by the forces of power history and yet survives and has an impact on world history, completely out of proportion to its numbers and its material power, proves the validity of another dimension of reality and testifies to God's "powerless" guidance in the affairs of men. Gods own destiny in history is linked to the history of Israel. Only by means of Israel may his, of necessity, unconvincing presence in history be surmised.

This is the ultimate significance of the idea of the chosen people. God needs a small and relatively weak people in order to introduce another dimension into history—human life—not by might nor by power but by His spirit. "The Eternal did not love you nor choose you because you were more numerous than any other people";[3] He could not associate his cause with the mighty and the numerous. It is not through them that a God who renders himself "powerless" in history, for the sake of man, can advance his purpose for man. Only a nation whose presence in and impact on history testify to God's presence may be God's people. God's relation to human history is such that he needs a chosen people. The chosen people satisfies a need for divine concern for all men. Why the Jews? No matter whom he would have chosen, they would have to become Jews. This idea of the divine need comes to expression in the passage in Isaiah to which we had occasion previously to refer. The concept of the witness is also stated in the following manner:

> Ye are My witnesses, saith the Eternal,
> And my servant whom I have chosen;
> That ye may know and believe Me, and understand
> That I am He;
> Before Me there was no God formed,
> Neither shall any be after Me.[4]

A careful reading of the text will show that Israel does not witness, nor was it chosen, because it knows, believes, and understands. On the contrary, it has been made the witness and has been chosen, so that it may know, believe, and understand. Out of his chosenness, from his own history he should learn to know, to believe, and to understand. He is the witness, whether he knows it or not, whether he consciously testifies or refuses to testify. His very existence, his survival, his impact, testifies to God's existence. That he is here, that he is present, bears witness to God's presence in history. He has been chosen for this purpose and he should have the moral courage to draw the consequences from his own function in history. Then he will know and he will learn to believe, and through faith will learn to understand.

2.

Jewish survival has confounded Israel's enemies and opponents and has been a source of disquieting puzzlement in the affairs of men. It is the great mystery of world history. The survival of a people that has lived without power is inexplicable in a world that lives essentially by reliance on power. A people without a country, without an organized government, without any of those resources of material power that alone seem to count in human history—whence its staying power, whence its stamina to preserve its identity? In the Christian dark and Middle Ages the mystery of Israel's survival was explained as the work of the devil: The Jew was in alliance with the Adversary, the Jew was satanic or Satan himself. Given the Christian premise, this was in a sense "logical." The Jew lived and endured by a strength unrecognized in Christendom. It was a strength unknown in Christian lands and therefore hidden and mysterious. If it was not of God, surely it must come from the Adversary. Given the Christian premise, there was some truth in the argument. Israel endured in the midst of Christendom in a manner that defied all the "Christian" requirements for survival in history. To discern in the feautres of the Jew the face of Satan was a Christian necessity of the dark and Middle Ages. It was the tragic recognition of God's people by the medieval Christian psyche. In more modern times, the "explanation" was not readily acceptable. The Satan of Christendom was replaced by the secret international conspiracy of the elders of Zion. This idea, however fantastic, also has a certain logic of its own. It acknowledges the fact that Israel's survival is not explicable in terms of the historical dimensions within which people normally live. It rightly surmises that there is a secret to which the mysterious survival power of this powerless nation is due. It is wrong in the identification of that secret. That, too, is understandable. For the secret is God's hidden presence in history. There is indeed a "secret world government" at work in history. It consists of God's power-divested guidance in history. Because it is "powerless" it is hidden; yet its reality is intimated in the inexplicable survival of God's people.

The most tragic testimony to this presence-in-absence is provided by the Nazi crime of Germany against Israel. The ferocity with which this crime was perpetrated represents the ultimate of irrationality. The conscious and radical removal of every vestige of moral restraint on subhuman passions, the limitless inhumanity, the calculated reversal of all human values and the extirpation of all human feelings, the ideology of hate and the religion of brutality pursued and practiced by the Germans was not "of this world." It had a quality of the transcendental about it; it was metaphysical barbarism. It was not just inhuman; it was satanic. Many millions perished at the hand of the Germans, but the satanic hatred of Nazi Germany was reserved for the Jews exclusively. In terms of "this world" the hatred is inexplicable. Nazi Germany was, indeed, afraid of Israel. The fear was utterly unjustified in terms of material or political power. Nothing could be more ridiculous than to imagine that there was any rational foundation for one of the great military powers of history to be afraid of the might of "world Jewry." Nothing could be further from the truth than the mad suspicion of a Jewish conspiracy against Germany. Yet, the fear was real; more real than any fear human beings may have of superior material or political forces that may be arrayed against them. It was a metaphysical fear of the true mystery of God's "powerless" presence in history as "revealed" in the continued survival of Israel. It was a well-justified fear. For the presence of the "powerless" God in history indeed spelled the doom of the Nazi-German rebellion against all universal human values from the very beginning. The rebellion had to be satanic because it was to dethrone God. The "hiding" God of history was a repudiation of everything Nazi Germany stood for. He was to be eliminated for all times. There lies the origin of the satanic idea of the Final Solution. If the symbol of this presence-in-absence were eliminated, if the witness were destroyed, God himself would be dead. The metaphysical quality of the Nazi-German hatred of the Jew as well as the truly diabolical, superhuman quality of the Nazi-German criminality against the Jew are themselves testimonies to the dark knowledge with which a nazified Germany sensed the presence in history of the hiding God. God is revealed in the midst of the hiddenness in the suffering of his people. At times, his enemies sense his hidden presence more actuely than those who are of his people.

No wonder that communist Russia is so much more anti-Jewish than it is anti-Christian. If it were only a matter of the antagonism of an atheistic society to religion, there should be no difference between communism's rejection of Christianity and that of Judaism. There is, of course, the ingrained traditional Christian antisemitism that the new Russia inherited from its czarist past. But this by itself is hardly sufficient to explain the ruthless oppression of Jewish religious and cultural life and the systematic closing of all avenues that might serve to preserve Jewish identity. Nor can it explain the revival of the Nazilike antisemitic propaganda in the authentic style of Streicher's *Stürmer* that is sweeping Soviet Russia these days. The key to the understanding of Soviet antisemitism may be provided by the case of Karl Marx, a man of Jewish parentage yet a venomous antisemite. The case of Marx cannot be explained by quoting the intellectual conflict between atheism and religion; it reaches much deeper. The whole materialistic interpretation of history stumbles over the reality of the Jew. The Jew as the witness to God's presence in history is a refutation of dialectical materialism. His existence, his survival, is not a theoretical refutation—that would be of little concern to the presently mighty communist empire—but a factual one. As long as the Jew is around he is a witness that God is around. And as long as God is around any purely materialistic civilization can only be a passing phase in history. The reality of the witness arouses the venom of those whose avowed purpose it is to build against God.

The case of Christianity, for instance, is rather different. Since the days that Christianity sold its soul to the sword of Constantine, its progress has been explainable in this-worldly terms. Its influence is due to its numbers. It is fully understandable within the power-political frame of reference; there is nothing mysterious, nothing strange about it. Power one can meet with greater power. But the Jew, he is the mystery. His survival capacity, his influence, his impact, are unrelated to his material strength. In terms of the world, as the Gentiles know it and dominate it, he is inexplicable. He is the mysterious stranger in world history. Yet, he is—exists and survives—and thus witnesses to another power, to another meaning, to another plan for man—to God.

The fear that so many different civilizations have of the Jew, the suspicion with which he is met, is utterly irrational, yet it has its justification. It is utterly irrational, because it has no basis in the behavior of the Jew or in his character. It is a form of international madness when it is founded on a belief in Jewish power and Jewish intention to hurt, to harm, or to rule. Yet it has its justification as a metaphysical fear of the staying power of Jewish powerlessness. The very existence of the Jewish people is suggestive of another dimension of reality and meaning in which the main preoccupations of the man of power history are adjudged futile and futureless in the long run. Israel's survival has a corollary in the judgment that is, sooner or later, executed in history notwithstanding God's silence. While God is long-suffering, he is not so forever. That would not be divine mercy, but divine indifference. Were there no judgment in history over power history, faith history would have no chance of survival. Israel has survived because of the world judgment that is also found in world history.

According to Jewish tradition, God originally planned to create the world according to his attribute of justice. But he saw that a world ruled by a just God could not exist. He, therefore, let his attribute of mercy precede and, thus, he associated mercy with justice and created the world.[5] What is not stated in the teaching but is implied, is the equally true thought that although it is sure that the world will not stand by divine justice, it is at least extremely doubtful that it could survive by unlimited divine mercy. For it is God's love and mercy that gives men the opportunity for satanic self-assertion and rebellion against God himself. Because of God's long-suffering, man may indulge in hubris and get away with it. But hubris too, if it remains unchecked; will destroy man. A world ruled by divine justice would perish because of God's justice; a

world ruled by divine mercy would perish because of human
hubris. A world of justice could not endure the divine wrath; a
world of pure divine long-suffering could not endure man's wrath.
There is judgment, but mercy precedes it. Judgment is delayed by
divine mercy and forebearance. Because mercy delays judgment,
man may indulge in rebellion and become guilty of hubris. Because
God is forebearing, man may get away with it for a while. But
judgment is only delayed. The man of hubris does not escape
nemesis. There is judgment and there is a Judge in world history.
The manner of Israel's survival testifies to the long-suffering Judge
of history.

GALUT

Galut, exile, seems to be the dominant feature of Jewish history.
The Jewish people have lived longer in exile than in their homeland
in Eretz Yisrael, yet *Galut* is considered an abnormal condition
both politically and spiritually. The Jew in the *Galut* is fenced
in on all sides, politically, socially, economically; his very life is
continually in jeopardy. The area too in which Judaism may grow
and live is narrowly circumscribed—it is largely limited to the
synagogue and the home. How did Jews understand their exile?
How did they explain it to themselves? They looked upon it as
part of the great dialogue between God and Israel. In the Books of
Moses, and later on by the prophets, they already were warned
that if they did not keep their covenant with God, the land would
"spew" them out and they would be scattered among the nations.
Indeed there exists a deep-rooted tradition that *Galut* is a punishment for sins. It is the old *Mipnei Hataeinu* (Because of our sins)
idea that we discussed earlier. It was not easy to maintain such
an idea. Exile has gone on much too long; the suffering was often
too heavy to bear. The questions were unavoidable: Are we so
much worse than the others? Are our transgressions so much
more grievous? A great deal of ingenuity was spent in order to
justify the idea of punishment. If one would wish not to lose faith
in the merices of the Almighty, one could take recourse in the
talmudic teaching that God is exacting of the righteous "up to a

hair-breadth." The righteous are judged much more strictly, because they ought to know better. One could also take refuge from the searching questions of threatening disbelief by recalling the words of Amos (3:2):

> You only have I known of all the families of the earth;
> Therefore I will visit upon you all your iniquities.[6]

Although, as we saw earlier, even in the Bible and the Talmud it was not accepted as the only satisfactory explanation, Jews through the ages clung to it stubbornly. It is understandable; there was solace in it. One could preserve one's self-respect and also retain ones faith in God's justice. Israel's very closeness to God explained Israel's destiny in exile.

Such ideas were supported by another trend in Jewish thought—the positive value of suffering. Rightly endured, suffering purifies and deepens the human personality. It induces man to turn inward; to foreswear the superficial pleasures of the passing moment and to concentrate on the enduring values of human existence, perhaps to seek ultimate meaning where alone it may be found—in a realm beyond time and space. The ideas were often helpful in the darkest hours of the *Galut*. They enabled the Jew to carry on, to move from catastrophe to catastrophe without surrendering either faith or hope. Indeed, after each catastrophe his spirit revived in faith, sure that suffering was the necessary phase preceding the coming of the Messiah. Jews could believe it because through suffering they had atoned for their sins, they were purified, they were tested and stood the test. Because of suffering they were ready for the Messiah, worthy of him. The periods of great crisis and persecution were usually the hour of the false Messiah. If the Messiah did not come, there was always an explanation. Somehow, Jews failed again. The explanation was not always convincing. The *Galut* had gone on too long, it was too cruel. In the numerous penitential prayers of the synagogue, the *S'lihot,* the question for the reason of it all, is recurring continually. It was summed up in a famous passage: "All exiles come to an end, only mine increases; all questions are answered, but my question returns ever to the place from which it came."[7]

Is there nothing but punishment, purification, and waiting only

to be disappointed? Needless to say, in the light of all that has
been said earlier in this essay there is also another approach to
the problem, more valid and equally well rooted in the teaching.
Exile as a single event may well be punishment. But exile as an
enduring condition, and entailing survival in spite of it, belongs to
a fundamentally different category. Usually, exile is understood as
a sequence, an abnormal phase following upon a normal one.
Galut, the specifically Jewish form of exile, is rather different: it
does not follow; it is at the beginning. Jewish history begins with
God's words to Abraham: "Get thee out of thy country, and from
thy kindred, and from thy father's house, unto the land which I
will show thee." [8] The history of Judaism commences with *Galut.*
If exile is at the very start then there must be something in the
nature of Judaism, in God's plan for the Jewish people, which is
inseparable from it. Abraham, in order to become the patriarch
of Israel, had to leave his father's house and the land of his birth.
He embraced his destiny in a world which was alien to him, to
his faith, to his values, to his truth. He went into exile, because
in the world as it existed then, Abraham could not find a home.
He had the choice: either to be true to himself and become a
stranger, or wanderer, or to become one with his surroundings and
remain at home. He chose himself, his own personal destiny; but
in order to do that he had to go into exile. Even before they were
born, it was decreed concerning his descendants that they would
be strangers in a land that was not theirs, where they would be oppressed and afflicted for four hundred years. [9] Obviously this could
not have been a punishment. The children of Israel, whom the
natural course of events had taken to Egypt, could have merged
with the Egyptian people and have been completely absorbed by
Egypt's civilization. But if they were to remain Jews and loyal to
the obligations of their descent, they had to remain apart. Again,
like their father Abraham, they had a choice: to surrender their
identity and submerge in the majority or to remain true to themselves and become strangers and live in exile.

What is the significance of *Galut* as a starting point? One might
generalize and say: There are certain ideals that are not easily
absorbed by the order of the world; there are values that are re-

pulsed by the laws of power history; ideas and values that are strangers among men and are of tragic necessity forced into exile. Such a stranger in history is the idea represented by the Jewish people in the history of mankind. The history of a people of God, a people that enters on the scene of history on the strength of a covenant with God, that sees its responsibility as a people to obey God's word and to do his will, must begin in a condition of *Galut.* As Abraham did not fit into the local world of his birthplace so do his children not fit into the universal world of the nations to the extent that it is dominated by materialistic self-interest and ambitions of power. We say in our prayers, "Because of our sins we have been exiled from our land," but the truth is that during the period of the Second Temple the Jewish people had already completely given up every form of idolatry. It was the period of the great teachers of the Mishnah. During that time Israel was probably closer to God than in any previous phase in its history. Yet, this generation was overtaken by the catastrophe of the *hurban,* the destruction of the Temple and the state and the scattering of the people into the four corners of the world. There was no metaphysical reason for this. What happened was quite natural. For in the world as it existed then, a world ruled by the Roman Empire, there was indeed no room for the people of the prophets, the people of a Hillel and a Rabban Gamliel.

There are many passages in Talmud and Midrash that describe God as weeping over the exile of his children.[10] This is in keeping with our earlier analysis that God, having created man, rendered himself "powerless" in a sense. Why should exile involve the kind of suffering Israel had to endure? It is taken for granted that a minority scattered all over the world that attempts to retain its identity will be oppressed and persecuted. But this can only be taken for granted because there is something very wrong with man and with the world. Whenever a minority is persecuted, justice, humanity, decency are all in a state of exile from the affairs of men. The case of the Jew is, of course, aggravated by the fact that, not by what he does, but by what he is, indeed by the fact that he is, represents a challenge to the principle by which nations "normally" live. And God himself is "powerless." He could crush

man and destroy man's world. But if he desires man, he must take
the risk with him and wait for him until man becomes what he
ought to be. This, of course, means that exile is a cosmic condition.
God himself is a refugee in the world. This is the final meaning
of the Jewish concept of *sh'khinta b'Galuta,* the Divine Presence
in exile in the world. The *Galut* of the Jewish people is a specific
case of this cosmic condition and a necessary outcome of it.

In spite of the suffering involved there is also majesty in exile,
the majestic loyalty of a people that in an unprecedented and
unparalleled manner has kept faith with an ideal. Even Jews are
often inclined to look upon their *Galut* as a phase of passivity
in which the Jewish people are a mere object for the butt end of
history. The truth is that their condition was a matter of choice.
But for the Nazi period, Jews could always escape persecution
through apostasy, by conversion, through assimilation and complete surrender of identity. The arms of Christianity, especially,
were always spread out invitingly toward the Jew. Because of the
daily pressures and persecutions, every day that the Jew endured
and remained loyal to his God or to his identity was a day of
choice and decision. To accept the day-by-day challenge and not
to surrender, no matter what the consequences, has been a deed
of the spirit that for intensity, duration, and willingness for self-
sacrifice remains unique in the history of mankind.

THE SUFFERING SERVANT OF GOD

If God is "powerless," God's people, too, will be powerless. To
be God's people is more than acknowledging God; it means accepting God's world in all its consequences for those who acknowledge Him. God's people may cry out in their agony: How long
still, O God! but will put up with God's long-suffering, with His
questionable experiment, man. To be chosen by God is to be
chosen for bearing the burden of God's long-suffering silences and
absences in history. It is for this reason that at the beginning of
Israel's history, stands the *Akedah,* the binding of Isaac. Abraham
was not guilty, nor was the sacrifice desired of him, punishment.
It was initiation into the sacrificial way of the Chosen Ones. What
was revealed to the patriarch was repeated as his children were

led onto the path that they were to take through history: "Know of a surety that thy seed shall be a stranger in a land that is not theirs, and shall serve them, and they shall afflict them four hundred years." [11] It was all decided before the child, destined to become father to the nation, was even born. It was repeated innumerable times later. God's chosen ones suffer guiltlessly. It is what is called in Hebrew terminology *gezeira,* an inscrutable divine decree. The decree is not that there be human suffering; the decree is that there be divine long-suffering with man in spite of man's criminal turpitude; indeed, the decree is that there be this world of man which could not stand without divine forebearance. Suffering of the guiltless is the indirect result of the decree of creation. The thought finds its moving expression in the awesome solemnity of the liturgy of the "Ten Martyrs," which is recited on the Day of Atonement. The very angels in heaven cried out bitterly: "Is this then the Torah? And this its reward?" Whereupon a heavenly voice was heard: "If I hear another sound, I shall turn the world back to water and my throne's footstool (i.e., the earth[12]) to *tohu v^a'bohu.* This is a decree *(gezeira)* from before me. Accept it ye who find your pleasure in the Law, which precedes the creation." Why did they not utter that one sound, that protesting No to the abomination, euphemistically called "the footstool of his throne"? If such is the footstool, by all means let it go crushing down into its primordial *tohu v^a'bohu!* The martyrs, Rabbi Akiba and his saintly friends, did not speak that condemning No. They knew that the real issue was not their suffering; at stake was God's act of creation, his freedom and authority to say, "Let there be!" The chosen ones know that the choice is between *tohu v^a'bohu* of non-existence and their acceptance of the yoke of the divine experiment of creation. Without their acceptance, the world would indeed have to be turned back into nothingness. Only when the chosen ones choose to accept "the decree" does the world acquire the moral right to continue to exist. As they accept the yoke, God may go on being long-suffering with the rest of mankind. The world is sustained by the suffering of the guiltless.

God's chosen people is the suffering servant of God. The majestic fifty-third chapter of Isaiah is the description of Israel's martyrology through the centuries. The Christian attempt to rob

Israel of the dignity of Isaiah's suffering servant of God has been one of the saddest spiritual embezzlements in human history. At the same time, the way Christianity treated Israel through the ages only made Isaiah's description fit Israel all the more tragically and truly. Generation after generation Christians poured out their iniquities and inhumanity over the head of Israel, yet they "esteemed him, stricken, smitten of God, and afflicted." At the same time, they misunderstood the true metaphysical dignity of the suffering of God's servant. What is the weight of one sacrifice compared to the myriads of sacrifices of Israel? what is one crucifixion beside a whole people crucified through centuries? But, it is maintained, the one crucified was a god, whereas the untold millions of Jewish men, women, and children were only human beings. Human beings only! As if the murder of an innocent human being were a lesser crime than the killing of a god. A god after all does not have to die. If he is killed, it is because he offers himself freely as a sacrifice. A god chooses to be killed; he knows what he is doing and why he is doing it. And when he dies, he does not suffer as a god. As a "very man" he suffers the agony of a single man. But the little boy who at the door of the gas chamber says to his mother: "But, Mama, I was a good boy!"[13] that is something quite different. That is crucifixion! Or the little boy of eleven pressed into the indignity of a cattle truck on its way to Treblinka. The endless journey in the heat of a burning summer. There is hardly any room to stand. Occasionally, one steps on a corpse who only moments ago was a neighbor, a friend, a loved one. There is no air, no water, no sanitary facilities; ultimate darkness and doom! The father beside him. "My little boy, whom I was holding by the hand was almost suffocating from lack of air and thirst. His legs were giving way under him; he was sagging to the floor. I had to support him. He spoke in his fever: Daddy! We are going to Mama. Aren't we? I do see her. Hie! Open the doors! Shoot us! An end! Let there be an end to it!" This too is something quite different. This is what I call crucifixion. Or the eight-year-old in the refugee center in the Warsaw Ghetto. The child is by now mad and runs around screaming: "I want to steal, I want to rob, I want to eat, I want to be a German." Such is crucifixion. And it has been suffered not by gods, but by human beings, endured again and again on innumerable occasions all through Jewish history in Christian lands. That deicide is the greatest of human crimes is among the most dangerous fallacies ever taught to man. The truth is that the capital crime of man is not deicide, but homicide. To torture and to kill one innocent child is a crime infinitely more abominable than the killing of any god. Had Christianity, instead of being preoccupied with what it believed to have been a deicide, concentrated its educative attention on the human crime of homicide, mankind would have been spared much horror and tragedy. There would have been much less suffering and much less sorrow among all men; nor could there have been either Auschwitz or Treblinka. Unfortunately, the teaching of deicide became an excuse, and often a license, for homicide. Pity any god thus caricatured by his devotees!

God suffers not on account of what man does to him. What could man do to God? He suffers because of what man does to himself and to his brother. He suffers the suffering of his servant, the agony of the guiltless. In all their affliction, he is afflicted.[14] In the liturgy of the High Holy Days, God is referred to as the one who suffers, as he averts his eyes from the rebellious. He is long-suffering with man and suffers with the victims of man who carry the burden of his long-suffering patience and mercy. How he must love those who suffer innocently because he cannot but bear even with those of his creatures who have failed him! God's servant carries upon his shoulders God's dilemma with man through history. God's people share in all the fortunes of God's dilemma as man is bungling his way through toward messianic realization. The status of the dilemma at any one moment in history is revealed by the condition of Israel at that moment. God's people is God's challenge to man. God, who leads man "without might and without power" sent his people into the world without the might of power. This is the essence of the confrontation between Israel and the world. It was in this confrontation that Western man had to prove himself. God has pushed Israel right across the path of Christianity. Israel was God's question of destiny to Christendom. In its answer, the Christian world failed him tragically. Through Israel God tested Western man and found him wanting. This gruesome failure of Christianity has led the Western world to the greatest moral debacle of any civilization—the holocaust.

THE WITNESS AFTER THE HOLOCAUST

1

Does all this justify God's silence during the European holocaust of the Jewish people or does it even explain it? As we have already stated it is not our intention to explain it, and certainly not to justify it. We have tried to show what is implied in Judaism's faith in the God of history independently of our contemporary experience. The question is, of course, well-grounded: Can such faith still be maintained in the face of the destruction of European Jewry? People of our day are often apt to give quick and mainly emotional answers to the question. This is understandable. We have been too close to the catastrophe, too deeply and personally involved. However, notwithstanding our deep emotional involvement, it is essential first of all to gain a clear intellectual grasp of the problem.

The Jewish, radical theologian of our day—and the numerous less sophisticated people whose preoccupation with the problem of Auschwitz does not let them reach any other solution but the negative one—do not understand the true nature of the quandary of faith that confronts us. The problem of faith here is a problem of theology in the broadest sense of the word. What becomes questionable is the manner in which God relates himself to the world and to man. Strictly speaking, the questioning of God's justice in his relation to history has little to do with the quantity of undeserved suffering. The enormity of the number of martyrs of our generation—six million—is not essential to the doubt. As far as our faith in an absolutely just and merciful God is concerned, the suffering of a single innocent child poses no less a problem to faith than the undeserved suffering of millions. As far as one's faith in a personal God is concerned, there is no difference between six, five, four million victims or one million. Nahmanides expressed the thought clearly in his *Sha'ar Ha'gmul* in the following words: "Our quest [regarding theodicy] is a specific one, about [the plight of] this particular man. . . . This problem is not reduced if those who fall are few in number; nor does it become more serious if their number increases. For we are not discussing [the ways of] man. . . . Our arguments concern the Rock, whose work is perfect and all His ways just; there is nothing perverse or crooked in them." [15] Nothing is easier than to miss, for emotional reasons, the decisive importance of such a statement. How can one compare the suffering of a few to that of a multitude? How dare one raise the problem over the death of one innocent child as one must over that of a million and a half innocent Jewish children slaughtered by the Germans! One cannot and one dare not—as long as one judges man. There is a vast difference between less injustice and more injustice, between less human suffering and more. One human tragedy is not as heartbreaking as the same tragedy multiplied a millionfold. A man who murders one person is not as guilty as a mass murderer. The German crime of the ghettos and concentration camps stands out in all human history as the most abominable, the most sickening, and the most inhuman. But justice and injustice, guilt and innocence are matters of degree only for man. When one questions the acts of an Absolute God, whose every attribute, too, is absolute by definition, the innocent suffering of a single person is as incomprehensible as that of millions, not because the sufferings of millions matters as little as those of one human being, but because with Him the suffering of the one ought to be as scandalous as that of multitudes. An absolute just God cannot be a tiny bit unjust. The least injustice in the Absolute is absolute injustice. An infinitely merciful God cannot be just a little bit unconcerned about innocent suffering. The least amount of indifference in the Infinite is infinite indifference. With Elisha ben Abuyah to have witnessed one case of undeserved suffering of the innocent was sufficient to raise the problem and cause him to lose faith. Such was also the insight of Camus. One compares the two sermons of the priest in *The Plague*. The first is a fire-and-brimstone preachment about the divine judgment that descended upon the sinful city; the second one is the mild acknowledgment of an impenetrable mystery. What happened between the two preachings? The priest had to witness the agony of a single child dying of the plague. One case was sufficient to change the man, who ultimately dies of the sickness of the incomprehensible.

Once the problem of evil is understood in its valid dimensions, the specific case of the holocaust is not seen to be essentially different from the old problem of theodicy.

It is still the old problem of Epicurus that confronts us. If God desires to prevent evil but is unable, he is not omnipotent. If he is able to prevent evil, but does not desire to do so, he is malevolent. If he is able and desires to prevent it, whence evil? The problem has been discussed by all thinking and believing people through the ages. It is one of the themes in Plato's *Statesman*. Already in those days there were those who from the presence of evil in the world concluded that God must be absent from history. He had to be far removed from the earthly scene; he could have no knowledge of man. If he did, how could he tolerate the evil that was done under the sun! This consideration was also one of the reasons for the assertion in later Aristotelianism that God had no knowledge of "singulars" and thus, divine providence was in no way concerned with the plight of the individual being or creature. These were the early forms of what in our days likes to call itself radical theology.

Once the questioning of God over the holocaust is motivated by the vastness of the catastrophe, the questioning itself becomes ethically questionable. It is of course more human to query God about the suffering of the many rather than the few, but it is certainly not more humane. On the contrary, it is more ethical, and intellectually more honest and to the point, to question God about the life and happiness of which even a single soul is being cheated on this earth than to base one's doubts and quest on the sacrificial abandonment of millions. With God the quantity of injustice must be immaterial. To think otherwise is itself a sign of callous indifference toward injustice and human suffering. To suggest that one could put up with less evil and less injustice, but not with so much, is cruelly unethical. Indeed, the holocaust was only possible because mankind was quite willing to tolerate less than the holocaust. This was the decisive aspect in the guilt of man in our times. It is important to understand the true nature of the problem if one involves God in it, questioning his ways with man and the world. It is the precondition for developing the attitude that may enable us to live meaningfully with the problem, even though its ultimate solution may forever escape us. Understood in its vastest intellectual dimension and its radical ethical relevance, the question is not why the holocaust, but why a world in which any amount of undeserved suffering is extant. This, of course, means that the question is tantamount to, why man? why a world of man? For, indeed, if man is to be as a being striving for value-realization, God must tolerate and endure him as a failure and an accusation.

How long is he to be tolerated as a failure, how long to be endured by God as an accusation of God? Who is to say! In order to answer the question, one ought to know the heart of God. How long God is willing to endure his creation even as a failure is the secret of creation itself. God's dominion over the world is not a dominion of justice.[16] In terms of justice, he is guilty. He is guilty of creation. But is he guilty of indifference or is he guilty of too much long-suffering? How vast is the infinitude of his mercy, his patience with man? When is it the moment for his justice to intervene and to call a halt to misused human freedom? Can we gauge the reach of his love even for the wicked, be they even those of his creatures who choose to become his failures? According to midrashic teaching, at the time of the drowning of the hosts of Pharaoh in the Red Sea the angels in heaven, as is their wont, were preparing to chant the daily hymn in praise of the Almighty. But God silenced them with the words: "The works of my hands are drowning in the sea and you sing my praises!"[17] It is not an easy matter for God to execute judgment over the guilty. Even "his failures" are the works of his hands.

2

The question after the holocaust ought not to be, how could God tolerate so much evil? The proper question is whether, after Auschwitz, the Jewish people may still be witnesses to God's elusive presence in history as we understand the concept. What of the nemesis of history and what of Jewish survival?

The Nazi crime of the German people attempted to eradicate the last vestiges of a possible innate sense of humanity, it sought the conscious extirpation from human nature of the last reminder of the fear of God in any form. It was the ultimate rebellion of nihilism against all moral emotion and all ethical values. However, this up to now mightiest and most morbid manifestation of human hubris too was overtaken by its complete and inescapable nemesis. In every field the very opposite of its goals has been accomplished. "Das Tausendjährige Reich," the empire for a millenium, was in ashes after twelve terrible years. Instead of the much heralded "Gross Deutschland" there is a divided Germany with greatly reduced frontiers. The nemesis is not limited to Nazi Germany alone, it has overtaken Western civilization itself. The holocaust is not exclusively the guilt of Germany; the entire West has a goodly share in it. One of the most tragic aspects of the world catastrophe of nazism is to be seen in the fact that it was able to assume its vast dimensions of calamity mainly because of the tolerance and "understanding" that it enjoyed in the world community of nations for many years. During the period of favorable international climate nazified Germany was able to create one of the most powerful war machines in all history, to poison the minds of vast sections of the world's population, and to corrupt governments and public officials in many lands. This was possible partly because, with the help of the antisemitic heritage of the West, Nazi Germany was able to bring about the moral disintegration of many peoples with diabolical efficiency and speed and partly—and not altogether independently of it—because of the cynical calculations of worldwide power politics. Germany was meant to become the bulwark of the West against the threat of Russian communism. To this end many were willing to ignore the German-Nazi challenge to elementary justice and humanity. After all, its worst venom was directed against the Jews only. Even after the second World War had already pursued its horrifying course in Europe for several years, there were still influential forces in the high seats of power, and even on the throne of so-called "spiritual grandeur," that hoped for a rapprochement between Nazi Germany and the Western powers. They thought it politically wise to go slow on Nazi-German criminality, piously hoping to bring off the brotherly alliance that would enable them to launch the greatest of all crusades, that against Soviet communism. Thus they became accomplices in the criminality of Auschwitz and the gas chambers. Nothing of what they had hoped for has been achieved.

Instead of a curbing of communism, for which Germany and her sympathizers hoped, communism has reached its widest penetration the world over. This is not stated with any partiality for communism, but solely from the point of view of an observer who tries to detect the functioning of nemesis in history. Nazi Germany could have been stopped early in its track had there been less indifference toward the plight of the Jews and a better understanding of the demoralizing power of antisemitism. But antisemitism had long been a respectable trait in Western civilization. Thus, the Second World War became inevitable, as a result of which all the formerly great powers of Europe had been reduced to second and third rank. And even Russia and the United States who came out of the war as superpowers dwarfing all others, what have they gained if, as a result of their overwhelming might, they render each other's future, as well as that of all mankind, rather questionable? It is no mere coincidence that having countenanced the Final Solution to the Jewish problem, partly with glee and partly with equanimity, the world is now confronted with the serious possibility of a Final Solution to the entire problematic existence of man on this planet. Every one of the ambitions that the forces of power history have been pursuing have been weighed and found wanting. Had the nations and their churches not been silent and indifferent to what was recognizably afoot in the early days of nazism, world history would have taken an entirely different course and mankind would not now be balancing on the very edge of the thermonuclear abyss. This post-holocaust era is charged with the nemesis of history. This is the ignoble twilight hour of a disintegrating civilization.

It is true the Jewish people had to pay a terrible price for the crimes of mankind and to-day, too, as part of mankind, they are themselves deeply involved in the crisis of the human race, yet the Final Solution intended for it is far from being final. Though truncated, Israel survived this vilest of all degradations of the human race. Not only has it survived, but rising from one of its most calamitous defeats, it has emerged to new dignity and historic vindication in the state of Israel.

The most significant aspect of the establishment of the state of Israel is the fact that Jews through the ages knew that it was to come. They were waiting for it during their wanderings for long and dark centuries. There was little rational basis for their faith in the eventual return to the land of their fathers. Yet they knew that one day the faith would be translated into historical reality. They lived with that faith in the sure knowledge of divine concern. For the Jew, for whom Jewish history neither begins with Auschwitz nor ends with it, Jewish survival through the ages and the ingathering of the exiles into the land of their fathers after the holocaust proclaim God's holy presence at the very heart of his inscrutable hiddenness. We recognized in it the hand of divine providence because it was exactly what, after the holocaust, the Jewish people needed in order to survive. Broken and shattered in spirit even more than in body, we could not have been able to continue on our Jewish way through history without some vindication of our faith that the "Guardian of Israel neither slumbers nor sleeps." The state of Israel came at a moment in history when nothing else could have saved Israel from extinction through hopelessness. It is our lifeline to the future.

3

Confronting the holocaust, the relevant consideration is the full realization that it does not preempt the entire course of Jewish history. One dare not struggle with the problem of faith as if the holocaust were all we knew about the Jew and his relation to God. There is a pre-holocaust past, a post-holocaust present, and there is also a future, which is, to a large extent, Israel's own responsibility. Auschwitz does not contain the entire history of Israel; it is not the all-comprehensive Jewish experience. As to the past, we should also bear in mind that the Jew, who has known so much of the "Hiding of the Face," has also seen the divine countenance revealed to him. Notwithstanding Auschwitz, the life of the patriarchs is still with him; the Exodus did not turn into a mirage; Sinai has not come tumbling down; the prophets have not become charlatans; the return from Babylon has not proved to be a fairy tale. It is, of course, possible for people to secularize the history of Israel and deny the manifestation of a divine presence in it. However, such secularization is independent of the holocaust. It is not very meaningful to interpret the entire course of Jewish history exclusively on the basis of the death-camp experience of European Jewry. If the believer's faith in Israel's "encounters" with God in history is false, it must be so not on account of Auschwitz, but because the "encounters" just did not happen. On the other hand, if these manifestations of the divine presence did occur, then they are true events and will not become lies because of the holocaust.

For the person who does not recognize the presence of God in the Exodus, at Sinai, in the words of the prophets, in innumerable events of Jewish history, Auschwitz presents no problem of faith. For him God is forever absent. Only the Jew who has known of the presence of God is baffled and confounded by Auschwitz. What conclusions is he to draw from this terrifying absence of divine concern? Is God indifferent to human destiny? But the Jew knows otherwise. He knows of the most intimate divine concern. Has God, perhaps, died? Is it possible that once upon a time there was a God who was not indifferent toward Israel, but that now something has happened to him, he has gone away, he is no longer? This is plain silly. It is possible for a human being to lose faith in God. But it is not possible for God to die. He either is and therefore, will ever be; or he is not and, therefore never was. But if God who was, is, and will ever be, is it possible that at Auschwitz he rejected Israel, he turned away from Israel as a punishment for its sins? To believe this would be a desecration of the Divine Name. No matter what the sins of European Jewry might have been, they were human failings. If the holocaust was a punishment, it was a thousandfold inhuman. The only crime of man for which such punishment might be conceivable would be the Nazi crime of Germany, and even there, one would hesitate to impose it.

The Jew of faith is thus left with the perplexing duality of his knowledge of God. He knows of the numerous revelations of the divine presence as he knows of the overlong phases of God's absence. Auschwitz does not stand by itself. Notwithstanding its unique position as perhaps the most horrifying manifestation of divine silence, it has its place in Jewish history beside the other silences of God together with the utterances of his concern. The Jew was called into being by the revelation of the divine in history.

It is because God allowed his countenance to shine upon man that he is what he is. Only because of that does he know of the absence of God. But thanks to that, he also knows that God's absence, even at Auschwitz, is not absolute. Because of that it was possible for many to know God even along the path to the gas chambers. There were many who found him even in his hiding. Because of the knowledge of God's presence, the Jew can find God even in his absence.

No, the holocaust is not all of Jewish history, nor is it its final chapter. That it did not become the Final Solution as was planned by the powers of darkness enables the Jew who has known of the divine presence to discern intimations of familiar divine concern in the very midst of his abandonment. This, too, is essentially an old Jewish insight.

Yet all this does not exonerate God for all the suffering of the innocent in history. God is responsible for having created a world in which man is free to make history. There must be a dimension beyond history in which all suffering finds its redemption through God. This is essential to the faith of a Jew. The Jew does not doubt God's presence, though he is unable to set limits to the duration and intensity of his absence. This is no justification for the ways of providence, but its acceptance. It is not a willingness to forgive the unheard cries of millions, but a trust that in God the tragedy of man may find its transformation. Within time and history that cry is unforgivable. One of the teachers of the Talmud notes that when God asks Abraham to offer him his son Isaac as a sacrifice, the exact rendering of the biblical words reads: "Take, I pray thee, thy son." [18] In the view of this teacher the "binding of Isaac" was not a command of God, but a request that Abraham take upon himself this most exacting of all God's impositions. In a sense, we see in this a recognition that the sacrificial way of the innocent through history is not to be vindicated or justified! It remains unforgivable. God himself has to ask an Abraham to favor him by accepting the imposition of such a sacrifice. The divine request accompanies all those through history who suffer for the only reason that God created man, whom God himself has to endure. Within time and history God remains indebted to his people; he may be long-suffering only at their expense. It was hardly ever as true as in our own days, after the holocaust. Is it perhaps what God desires—a people, to whom he owes so much, who yet acknowledge him? children, who have every reason to condemn his creation, yet accept the creator in the faith that in the fullness of time the divine indebtedness will be redeemed and the divine adventure with man will be approved even by its martyred victims?

THE NEMESIS OF POWER HISTORY

We realize that after all is said the question might be asked: Agreeing that the survival of the Jew and the emergence of the state of Israel are in intimation of God's hidden presence in history, how much has really been accomplished by either or both events? Looking at the world today, what impresses one most at a first glance is the emergence of vast power blocks, like the United States, the Soviet Union, and the People's Republic of China. States and countries like the British Empire, France, and Germany, which only a few decades ago were mighty and influential on a universal scale, have been reduced to second- and third-rate powers. Today, Jews may well ask themselves the question: What is the significance of Israel, the people and the state, on the world scene in the context of present-day world history? History has become the battleground of giants. What does a small people like the Jews amount to in a world dominated by a few colossi of overwhelming might and power?

The question is induced, in particular, by the rise of the state of Israel. Through the ages Jews longed for it and hoped for it. When the state was finally created, it was the culminating triumph of Jewish survival through the darkest experiences of human history. Yet, one cannot help pondering the question: Coming, as it did, in the atomic age, did not—perhaps—the state of Israel come too late? What a difference it would have made to millions of Jews, who perished in pogroms and concentration camps, what a difference to the entire position of the Jewish people in the world today, had the establishment of the state of Israel come one or two centuries sooner! In earlier days, the Jewish Problem held a major position in the Zionist analysis of the Jewish situation. The problem was seen as the homelessness of the Jewish people. It was believed that national sovereignty in the ancient homeland was the solution. However, in this age of the colossi, how much security is to be derived even from national sovereignty in a small state like Israel? We realize today that a state of this kind, notwithstanding its remarkable achievements and the industry and bravery of its citizens, may not be more secure than was the individual Jew during his long exile. In the world of giants, a state, too, may be "homeless."

The question as to the significance of the Jew in the context of present-day world history may of course be raised even more poignantly as regards the position of the Jew in the rest of the world. From the ancient lands of Jewish history on the European continent, Jews have been eliminated as a source of any kind of influence. In Soviet Russia, Jewry and Judaism lie prostrate under the heavy yoke of communism. Only on the American continent, and chiefly in the United States, does a large Jewish center exist whose members, enjoying the freedom of citizenship in a great democracy, take their place—and may make their mark—in every field of human endeavor. But notwithstanding the Jewish position on the American continent, it is extremely doubtful that any significant role may be ascribed to the Jew in the broader context of present-day human history. As the result of the radical transformations that have taken place the world over in our generation, all the major issues of human existence, issues of politics, economics, technology, human welfare and progress have become more and more universally comprehensive. They are dominated by the Universal powers: the power blocks of the atomic giants and the explosive energy of the vast population blocks like China and the African and South American continents.

The world is being organized in global terms. What is the significance of the Jew in this global phase of human history? About a generation ago, the German historian Theodor Mommsen called the Jews and Judaism the ferment of history. Has the Jew now become a *quantité négligeable,* a negligible quantity on the world scene?

So it would seem, at first glance, if we evaluate the world transformation in quantitative terms only. However, looked at from the angle of a qualitative interpretation, there is yet another view which presents itself to the observer. The emergence of the colossi also illustrates the futility of power as an arbiter of history. In our days it has become a commonplace to state that man, having amassed so much power that he is able to destroy life and civilization on a global scale, must learn to renounce power as a means of ordering or controlling relations between people and nations. It is true that at the moment the potential of sheer physical force is used as a deterrent and peace is preserved by a balance of terror. Quite clearly, however, such a situation cannot continue indefinitely. The collossi's fear of each other is a very shaky foundation on which to erect a lasting peace. If that is all on which man may base his hope for the future, there is little ground for optimism. In such a situation, the delicate balance of terror is bound to break down sooner or later and bring in its wake the dreaded universal conflagration. The inescapable demand of the historic moment requires the honest renunciation of material force in the dealings of the nations and power blocks with each other. But the honest and wholehearted renunciation of the use of power and might implies a genuine embracing of ethical and moral principles for the ordering of the life of all mankind. This is no longer mere sermonizing; it has become the "iron law" in this new phase of global history. Be decent or perish!

From the point of view of a philosophy of history the present phase offers an intriguing phenomenon. Man has known for a long time that the use of force against man was evil. But how was force to be defeated in history? By the use of greater force. Thus, mankind was caught in a vicious circle. Every defeat of power led to the rise of more power. And more power only intensified the power competition between the nations. In our days, history teaches us the solution to the problem: force is being weeded out of history by its own surfeit. Whereas in former times what nations could do with power induced them to use it, today the very immensity of power gathered in human hands compels man to surrender its use against his fellow man. Power has overreached itself and, thus, it has defeated itself. Philosophically speaking, this is a rather amusing phase in the dialectic of history. For some time now Marxists have been declaiming about the iron laws of dialectical materialism. One phase follows upon another in an inescapable sequence of necessity: slavery, feudalism, capitalism, and the ultimate culmination, communism. Each phase carries within itself the seeds of its own disintegration; each phase perishes of its own surfeit. In a sense, this was a rejection of the Jewish concept, as formulated by the prophet: "Not by might, nor by power, but by My Spirit, saith the Lord." Dialectical materialism denied any influence to the spirit, to ideas and ideals. Today, the dialectics of history is carrying mankind into a phase in which, "but by My Spirit," is no longer an ideal, but practical politics, the basic requirement for human survival. Dialectical materialism has suffered its own dialectical defeat. The scientific and technological transformation of the human situation demands the spiritual reformation of man and nations. It is the irony of history that, when materialism has reached one of its greatest triumphs—in world-embracing capitalist and communist power blocks—it has been outmaneuvered by a higher dialectics of the spirit.

It is, of course, true that mankind as a whole is psychologically not yet prepared for the dialectical need of survival by the might of the spirit. The present moment follows upon an age of materialism of the capitalist as well as the communist brand, of disenchantment, of the surrendering of ideals, of "the death of God," of cynicism and despair. For quite some time yet man will have to survive by the balance of terror, if he is to survive at all. However, the significance of our age as the dialectical self-defeat of physical force remains unaffected by the lack of human understanding.

The meaning of the world transformation, as it has taken place in this generation, is to be recognized as the task, imposed upon mankind today, to render the Spirit effective as a history-making force. Only because such is the nature of the challenge that confronts man in this hour is there any point in inquiring into the role destined for the Jew in this new phase of human history. One should have thought that the Jew was ideally suited, both by temperament and historical experience, for the task that faces mankind. Has he not survived because of the truth of the words, "but by My Spirit"? Has he not proved by his very survival that "My Spirit" is indeed a determining factor in history? Has he not

proved it long before the present dialectical self-defeat of might
and power in this atomic age? In his *The Meaning of History*
Nicolas Berdyaev wrote the following about the meaning of Jewish
history:

> I remember how the materialist interpretation of history, when I
> attempted in my youth to verify it by applying it to the destinies of
> peoples, broke down in the case of the Jews, where destiny seemed
> absolutely inexplicable from the materialistic standpoint. And, indeed,
> according to the materialistic and positivistic criterion, this people ought
> long ago to have perished. . . .[19]

One might say that the new historical situation requires of mankind what God demanded of the Jew from the beginning. Mankind
is entering upon its "Jewish era" or else upon an era of self-immola-
tion. As in the past so today, we are a nation without power. But
how strange are the ways of the God of history who has led mankind to a juncture where it too will survive as Jews have survived
to this day—by the renunciation of force as the arbiter of human
destiny! How mysterious are His ways that have turned the specific
Jewish stance in history into an inescapable universal necessity!
How wonderous the plans of God with Israel that this vindication
has come about immediately after the historical position of Israel
had received its most shattering blow! Auschwitz has tragically
dramatized the meaning of the new era that has broken in upon
mankind. In our days, man has concentrated in his own hand
adequate physical force to bring about the final solution to all
of man's problems in one apocalyptic world conflagration. The
holocaust has shown that man's lack of moral force is sufficient to
bring about such a "final solution." For what was proved by the
holocaust is not what man was capable of doing to the Jew, but
what man is capable of doing to his fellow. The bomb has rendered
the final solution on a universal scale a practical possibility; Auschwitz has demonstrated it to be morally feasible. The holocaust has
presented man with the issue of all issues that looms on the horizon
as mankind enters upon this new era. Not only has nazism been
discarded upon the rubbish heap of history, but so has any system
of society or government that seeks to triumph by force on a
worldwide scale. The global powers are like men deified in terms
of might. They are omnipotent. Yet, from now on they will have

to function in history not unlike God's own functioning as we see it described in the traditional terms of the Talmud: "Such indeed is His mightiness that He subdues his omnipotence and grants long-suffering to the wicked. And such is the proof of His awesomeness; for were it not for the fear of Him, how could one people survive among the nations!" [20] Now that mankind as a whole has entered upon the perilous destiny that till now has been reserved for Israel, the global powers, our earthly gods of history, will have to act in a manner following the example of the Divine Ruler—hiding their omnipotence, subduing it, and treating each other and the smaller nations with "long-suffering," even though "the other" may seem to each of them to be "the wicked one." When man himself reaches the goal of quasi omnipotence, true might consists in the self-control of such omnipotence, in the renunciation of its use. From now on mankind will survive by the same critical minimum of what in religious language we call "the fear of God" by which the Jewish people were able to survive to this day. From now on, *imitatio dei* is no longer a mere religious idea, but the practical requirement of human survival. The quasi-omnipotent man must, as if, absent himself from history, as the omnipotent God is wont to do.

The universal significance of both Jewish survival and the return of the Jewish people to their ancestral land should be understood in the context of the new era which mankind has reached. Jews have survived as a homeless people through the long centuries, without political might and significant material power, while mankind pursued the illusion that human destiny is to be determined by exactly those factors which the Jewish people were lacking. They have survived, witnessing again and again the nemesis of mere material power, into the world era when the Jewish affirmation has become a necessity for universal survival. Similarly, the return of the Jewish people to its ancient homeland should be seen in a historical context. This hour, in which man has ascended to the pinnacle of material power, is also the hour of his deepest moral and spiritual exhaustion. Because of the surfeit of power and the exhaustion of the spirit everything is in jeopardy. Quite clearly, the wave of the future is with neither of the power colossi of the moment. If either of them should insist on forcing the future of man in its own likeness, the world will be left only with the shambles of an inglorious past.

The immensity of the possibilities for "the works of peace" which are inherent in this great power and which, in the present world situation, is also wrought with ultimate peril, has already rendered archaic both giants, capitalism and communism, as modes of coping with the challenges that confront man. The foundations on which they arose have sunk away into the depths of past time. The historic moment calls for a civilization that surpasses both. The universal significance of Israel's return to the land of the fathers we see in the fact that it has taken place after the holocaust, i.e., in this hour of universal spiritual exhaustion and universal need for a spiritual rebirth of man. The restoration of Jewish sovereignty in Zion is not a goal in itself. What could be the political significance of a little Jewish state in the world of today! Political sovereignty is only the framework within which this remarkable people of history may lead its life according to its own vision and create a culture whose essential resources can only be of the spirit. That the relevance of that creation for mankind need not be proportionate to the political and material size of Israel has been sufficiently proven by the past history of the Jewish people and of the world.

CHAPTER VI

IN ZION AGAIN

1

When in the early spring of 1967 we decided to set down our thoughts on the problem of faith raised by the European holocaust, we could not anticipate that by the time the task was brought to a conclusion, a threat, in its consequences even more fateful than Auschwitz itself, would becloud the skies of Jewish existence. The Arab nations resolved to wipe the small state of Israel off the map of the earth. If the threat in all its seriousness could in no way have been surmised, the fact that the frightening drama of perhaps ultimate extinction would find its redemptive denouement in the awe-inspiring return of the Jewish people to Zion and Jerusalem could not have been visualized by the wildest imagination as being within the realm of historical possibilities. We started our discussion with the theological and religious problems arising from the darkest hour in the history of Israel's exile. Soon after our task was finished, we stepped into the brightest hour that God, in His unexpected mercy, bestowed upon Israel since the inception of its dispersion. But, of course, that is the question. Was it indeed "from God"? Was it in truth—to use the phrase of Isaiah—the "hiding" God of Israel who acted as the savior? How are the events and the results of Israel's Six-Day War to be seen in the context of the position we have tried to develop in the previous pages? Did we really experience one of those rare occasions, when God—almost as in biblical times—made his presence manifest as the Redeemer of Israel?

It was probably helpful that what we had to say on the problem of the European holocaust was developed independently of the impact of the Israeli victory. If our analysis of the Jewish affirmations in the face of the challenge of Auschwitz is valid, it must be so independently of Jewish military victories. On the other hand, if our analysis has no validity, no feat of arms, however magnificent, could change that. Military victory alone does not prove divine involvement in history, just as the crematoria are no proof of divine indifference. Defeat and suffering need not mean being abandoned by God and worldly success in the affairs of man is no proof of divine support. Nevertheless, the Jew the world over, and especially in the state of Israel, experienced the speedily developing crisis, followed by the lightening transformation of the Six-Day War as history on a metaphysical level. This was not a conscious reaction to what had happened; not an interpretation of the events, nor a considered judgment. As a conscious reaction, the sensing of metaphysical meaning might be questioned. But the realization that through the events of those few days all Israel was addressed from beyond the boundaries of time was not in the realm of conscious reaction. It was a spontaneous experience, born in upon the Jew with the power of inescapable revelational quality. Can this revelational character of the experience be proved? Revelation is never provable. One can only testify to its occurrence: Ye are my witnesses! says God. Once again the words of Isaiah have found their realization in world history. Nevertheless, after the event it is incumbent upon us to render account of the experience in the context of Judaic teachings and expectations. In order to do this we might do well to recall the theological relevance of a state of Israel, to examine the place that a Jewish state holds within the system of Judaism.

A vital aspect of Jewish messianism is the faith in Israel's return to its ancestral land. All the prophets that prophecy concerning Israel's redemption see it materialize in the land of Israel. God comforts Zion through the return of her children. Nothing could be further from the truth than to interpret these messianic hopes as a nationalistic aspiration. The prophetic mood belies such misconceptions. The messianic goal is a universal one. The Messiah ushers in universal justice and world peace. But the universal expectation is inseparable from Israel's homecoming. The very passage that directs man's hope to the time when "nation shall not lift up sword against nation, neither shall they learn war any more" also envisages that "out of Zion shall go forth Torah and the word of God from Jerusalem." [1] There can be little doubt that Zion and Jerusalem have no mere symbolical significance in this universalistic text, but are historic places in the land of the Jews. The prophets look forward to a time when God's plan for mankind is fulfilled, when peace and brotherhood prevail among all nations, when God's blessing embraces "Egypt My people and Assyria the work of My hands, and Israel Mine inheritance." [2] But the realization of all these expectations will find Israel reestablished in the land of its ancestors. The redemption of mankind includes the redemption of the Jewish people in the land of the Jews. Wherein lies the messianic significance of the land? The question is identical with the subject of our inquiry into the theological relevance of *Eretz Yisrael.*

2

The rabbis in the Talmud dared declare that a Jew who lives outside the holy land is to be considered as if he were an idolater. [3] This rather startling pronouncement flows from their understanding of Judaism. It is a statement concerning one of its essential qualities. It links the importance of the land not so much to the Jew as to the realization of Judaism. The question is often asked: what is the meaning of the term, "Jewish"? Is it a religious determination or does it apply to a national or racial entity? Formulated in this manner, the question cannot be answered. The frame of reference within which the question is asked does not apply to the Jewish people. The concepts "religion," "nation," "race," have their meaning and connotation which derive essentially from the tradition and history of the Western world. But Judaism does not derive its essential quality either from that tradition or from that history. The term "Jewish" is neither a religious nor a national concept. Yet, being Jewish does mean belonging to a people. Israel is a nation. But what kind of a people and nation? What kind of a people is it that has preserved its identity under conditions that no other people was ever able to maintain itself? What kind of a nation that though through the longest part of its history was lacking all the vital requirements of normal nationhood, yet was impressively discernable as a separate entity? One of the great Jewish teachers of the tenth century, Saadia Gaon, answered the question by saying: "Our people is a people only through the *Torah*." He was stating that it was the *Torah* that made Israel a people. Israel is a *Torah* nation. A nation created in its encounter with God; a nation formed by its faith, by its submission to the will of God as made manifest in the *Torah*.[4] Whatever the findings of anthropological science may say about the origins of the Jewish people, it has a bearing only on the raw material, as it were, out of which Israel was formed. The historical Israel came into being, and maintained itself through all times, as the result of its self-understanding as the people of God, the people of God's *Torah*. The formulation of Saadia Gaon defines in Jewish terms the meaning of Judaism as a religion and that of Israel as a people. Judaism is a nation-creating religion and Israel is a people created by this kind of a religion.

As a rule, religions do not make nations. Nations and peoples are biological, racial, political units. They will accept a religion but the religion they accept is accidental to the national group. Christianity, for instance, created no people; peoples, already existing as such, accepted Christianity. The same applies to the other world religions. Israel alone is a people made to fulfill a God-given task in history; the people whom, as Isaiah expressed it, God "formed" for himself.[5] Normally, religion follows nationhood; for the Jew his peoplehood flows from his religion. This is not only historically true, describing the emergence of Israel; in a sense it is valid to this day. An Englishman might accept Hinduism or Buddhism in London; it will not make him an Indian nor a Burmese. He will remain an Englishman. Similarly, a Chinese, converting to Christianity in China, does not become a European, a German, nor a Frenchman. But let the same people accept Judaism, not just pro forma, but in fact, living it and practicing it, they will become not merely adherents of a religion, but will belong to the Jewish people. The founder of Judaism was not a prophet, but a patriarch; the man of faith, by the intrinsic necessity of his faith, became the father of a people. On the rock of his faith he built, not a church, but a people that was to enter history with a God-invested purpose.

One may also put it this way. A key concept of Judaism is the idea of the covenant with God. In terms of the covenant one might say that whereas in other religions the "covenant" is between the individual and his God, in Judaism the covenant with the individual derives from the larger covenant with the group, the people. The covenant with an individual or a group of individuals constitutes the Jewish people. This, however, leads us to the essential distinction between what is traditionally understood by religion and the nature of Judaism. The concern of religion is with the right belief, the credo. Especially in the realm of Christianity, it is the right belief that establishes a correct relationship between the believer and his God. Judaism's main concern is with the deed. In keeping with the words of Habakkuk[6] Judaism does not teach that a man is *saved* by his faith but that the righteous *lives* by his faithfulness. In Judaism the significance of faith lies in its capacity to lead to life, to action, to the human deed. In one place in the Talmud the question is discussed: What is more important? The teaching or the deed? And the conclusion is reached: the teaching is more important, if it leads to the deed.[7] The deed, uninformed by the teaching, is blind; teaching that does not issue into the deed as a consequence is empty. The goal is the deed, guided by the teaching.

We may now be in a position to appreciate why the covenant in Judaism had to institute a people. One might say that the difference between Judaism and religion is due to the difference between deed and faith, between teaching-informed action and faith-conditioned salvation. Belief or faith belong in the private realm. The creed is always the credo of the individual. This is the reason religion does not create nations. Even if everyone in a people acknowledges the same religion, the relation thus established is not between the people as such and God, but between individuals and their God. The religion remains accidental to the national group.

A nation's historical role is enacted on a level different from the realm of the individual religious confession. The deed, however,

always takes place in the public realm. Faith is entertained in isolation. Indeed, the deeper the faith, the more private it is. The deed
is impossible in isolation. It always affects others, it impinges on
their lives, it always refers beyond the boundaries of isolated indi-
viduality. Faith is the preoccupation of the soul. The deed is enacted by the entire person. Faith links the soul to God; the faith-
informed deed links the whole person to the fellow man by way
of God. Faith fills the soul; the deed, history. While by faith alone
a soul may be saved, perhaps, the deed's *raison d'être* is to be
effective in the world. For the sake of its effectiveness, the deed
will seek for its realization a group that is moved by a common
faith and uinted by a common cause. The extent of the group
depends on the area within which the deed is to be enacted. (The
trade-union idea, for instance, concerns itself with a specific seg-
ment of the socio-economic structure of a society. In order to
issue into effective action, it must call into being the group that is
appropriate for its realization.) So it is with every idea that aspires
to enter the world in the form of the human deed. The boundaries
of the group will be determined by the area that the deed aims
to occupy. But what if the fruition of the idea as the deed en-
compasses the whole of human existence? if the faith seeks realization in economics, morals, politics, in every manifestation of
human life? In that case, the group ought to be all-comprehensive.
Such a group should be mankind.

But mankind is not a group; it is not a historical entity. Mankind
itself is an idea, an ideal. The comprehensive group to be created
to suit the comprehensive deed as a historical reality is a people in
sovereign control of the major areas of its life. The faith of Judaism
requires such a comprehensive deed. Realization through and within
the all-comprehensive collective, mankind, is the ideal; the instrument of its realization in history is the people. Since our concern
is with the comprehensive deed of Judaism, the people is Israel.
Of necessity, the covenant had to create the people with which the
covenant was concluded.

If, however, the people of Israel is the instrument of realization,
there must be a land of Israel as the place of realization. There
must be a place on earth within which the people are in command
of their own destiny, where the comprehensive public deed of

Judaism may be enacted. Individuals may live in two cultures; but no distinctive culture may grow and flourish authentically in an area already preempted by another one. The individual Jew may well find a home in any democratic society; Judaism must remain in exile anywhere outside the land of Israel. Outside the land of Israel Judaism is capable of partial realization only. The decisive fields of human endeavor are of course under the control of the dominant majority culture or civilization. The raw material, the challenge of the fullness of the human condition, is lacking. The Jewish deed cannot be enacted in the comprehensive dimension. Broad aspects of Jewish teaching must remain mere book learning for lack of applicability. Value concepts and standards degenerate into pious intentions starved of all relevance because, in the circumstances of Judaism's exile, they cannot become policy principles for the comprehensive deed of a Jewish people. According to the Bible, Moses was not granted the privilege of entering the promised land. Being informed of the divine decree, he prayed: "Let me go over . . . and see the good land. . . ." [8] One of the teachers in the Talmud, interpreting Moses' prayer in the midrashic manner, commented; "Why did our teacher Moses desire to enter *Erets Yisrael?* Was it so important for him to eat of its fruits and be satiated with its good things? But he thought: "There are numerous commandments that Israel was given by God which can only be fulfilled there. Let me go over that they may be fulfilled through me." [9] This comment expresses clearly the theological significance of the land. The teachers of the Talmud could not entertain the idea that Moses' interest in the land could have been of a secular nature. It could not have been due either to a wish for an easy life or to "patriotic" or nationalistic aspirations. The land was the opportunity of Judaic realization. The Torah is not fully applicable outside of the land of Israel. The consequences may be most serious. The non-application leads to continuous frustration of the spirit. The book learning, which is never tried in the midst of the contesting claims of live issues, withers. Judaism loses its creativity and is doomed to stagnation.

Those Jews who attempt to separate Judaism from Zion, Torah from the land of Israel give up both Torah and the land. Judaism without its chance for wholeness in fulfillment is a spiritual tragedy.

For the longest period of its history Jews have lived with it. But to embrace the tragedy as a desired form of Jewish existence is a forgery, a falsification of the very essence of Judaism. Those who sever Zion from the Torah have severed Judaism from its authentic sphere of realization. Thus, they have surrendered, as a matter of principle, Judaism's raison d'être, i.e., fulfillment in history. They have transformed its character by allowing it to sink to the level of a mere religion. They have reduced it to a credo, prayers of worship, and some home customs. All this may well be accompanied by good intentions and fine resolutions of a general humanitarian nature, but the unique significance of the Judaism of history will have been abandoned. What historically has been an obligation upon a public conscience and a standard for the public deed becomes relegated to the infinitely narrower scope of private creed and individual behavior. This is not reformation of a classical heritage but its planned decadence. What has essentially been a religious civilization is thus stripped down to a not very exciting creed, whose main function is to be a sedative in moments of trouble and visitation. The original way of life, derived from the challenge to build this world as a Kingdom of God, is turned into a gadget for securing peace of mind for the individual, a function which it is found to fulfill less and less effectively as this kind of religion declines.

Apart from the falsification of the very essence of Judaism, the severance of the land from the faith brings in its wake a drastic reevaluation of Jewish history. All through the ages Jews struggled, prayed, lived and died in the all-pervasive conviction that the meaning of their function in history would ultimately be revealed through their return to Zion. Jews were prepared to die at the stake because they knew that the final reckoning was not yet; and in our own days myriads of Jews perished in the gas chambers finding their only sustenance in their "perfect faith" in the coming of the Messiah. Basically, Jewish messianism has never been either a matter of politics or an expression of mere nationalism; it is a manifestation of the essence of Judaism. It is the faith in the inevitable triumph of the divine purpose in history that in the course of its unfolding would cause Israel to return to the holy land and there, in the fullness of its public life, embody Judaism.

From the very beginning, Judaism contained within itself the likelihood of exile as well as the certainty of redemption from exile. To be a Jew meant to accept the one and to wait for the other. Seen in this light, Jewish history does make sense: it is part of the cosmic drama of redemption. In it the massive martyrdom of Israel finds its significance: nothing of the sorrow and the suffering was in vain, for all the time the path was being paved for the Messiah. Not a single tear was wasted, for all of it will be vindicated in his coming. Only messianic redemption can lend meaning and bring justification to Israel's martyrdom. Thus must the authenticity of the Redeemer be tested: should he save only a contemporary generation, and compel the Jewish people to write off the tragedy of two millenia in exile as a regrettable incident about which nothing more can be done, Israel will know him to be another impostor. In a sense, every generation is the guardian of all generations, seeking and acknowledging only salvation of a kind that would redeem all Jewish history from the curse of a senseless martyrdom. Jews who desire to believe that the return to Zion and Jerusalem is not vital for Judaism have broken the continuity of Jewish history; they have given up Jewish messianism, and thus allowed the awesome drama of redemption to sink to the level of meaningless misery. The prophets, the martyrs, the numberless millions of simple people who perished believing and hoping, were all mistaken; the blood and the tears were all in vain: the Messiah has changed his destination and landed at New Amsterdam. This is the inherent logic of the falsification of the nature of Judaism. If Judaism is made into a purely private creed, not requiring collective implementation in the public life of the Jewish people, then indeed the two thousand years of Galut have been a deplorable episode, due to unfortunate circumstances, and the sooner it is forgotten the better for all.

3

Without return to Zion, Judaism and Jewish history become meaningless. The return is the counterpart in history to the resolution in faith that this world is to be established as the Kingdom of God. The thought has its roots in the very foundations of

Judaism, but might have been mere wishful thinking had it not
been supported by the reality of Israel, its existence, its survival,
its return to Zion. One must appreciate the irrationality of it all,
before one can grasp its significance. In terms of exclusively man-
made history, Israel's existence is irregular—a people like that of
the Jews is not supposed to exist; its survival, anomalous—a people
as irregular as the Jews is not expected to survive; its return to
Zion, absurd—the irregular and the anomalous compounded into
the impossible realization of a delusion. The Jew cannot stop at
this point. In terms of exclusively man-made history, which is the
same as Camus's exclusively man-made meaning, human existence
in general is a chance event in the midst of the anomaly of an
absurd universe. To be adjudged irregular, anomalous, and absurd
by the standards of a form of reality which is itself rather ridiculous is quite encouraging. In a human condition in which history
is altogether man-made, the historical Israel is an impossibility.
Yet, Israel is real. It can be real only because history is enacted
on a twofold level: it is man-made, the Kingdom is man's responsibility; it is God-planned, because the Kingdom of God on earth is
man's responsibility it may be delayed by crematoria and death
camps, yet come it must, come it will, a-coming it is. The movement of the two levels towards each other is the messianic process
of history. Israel is the only people that as a nation lives on both
levels. Israel's history is messianic history. For Israel history is
messianism on the way to the Kingdom of God on earth. Because
of that Israel knows Auschwitz, because of that Israel, all through
its history, has been on the way to Zion.

In our days it has arrived there. It may very well be that a
majority of the contemporary generation of Jews may not consciously subscribe either to our interpretation of Judaism or to that
of the Kingdom of God, yet the overwhelming majority of them
experienced the recent confrontation between the state of Israel
and the Arab nations as a moment of messianic history. It was an
event not on the purely man-made level of history, but one that
took place in conformity with the divine plan. Especially in the
land of Israel the widest section of the population were convinced
that "this is God's doing; it is marvelous in our eyes." [10] What
justification was there to see events in such a light? Apparently,

those who lived through them could not see them in any other. Generals and commanding officers were unable to render a purely military account of what happened. It was the secularist in Zion who insisted that not to recognize the miraculous would not be realistic. People who never prayed were overwhelmed by the desire to turn to God in prayer. It was not the prayer in the trenches where, supposedly, there are no atheists. It was the prayer beyond the trenches, in the clear air of victory; no prayer of fear, but prayer in its pristine spontaneity, as the elementary desire of the soul to reach out to God. The Jew has found himself. Hard-boiled paratroopers were embracing the cold stones of the West Wall of the ancient temple as lovers embrace the most beloved. There was a Presence about in the land. What is there in those events of unique Jewish destiny that we are able to discern from afar?

For the first time since the destruction of the ancient Jewish commonwealth the City of David is once again the capital of a Jewish state. Undoubtedly this is a moment in Jewish history that takes its place besides the classical occasions as recorded in the Bible. For the Jew this is a renewal of biblical times. The revelational impact of the event is undoubtedly partly due to the fact that it came upon us with the blow of the utterly unexpected. What happened was unplanned. The great powers could have easily prevented the outbreak of hostilities. Instead, they disregarded their moral responsibility and wasted the opportunity of peace making in foolish recriminations and idle chatter. Though the leader of the Arab camp threatened massacres that would surpass those of Genghis Khan, it is conceivable that he did not intend to go all the way. Israel wanted peace and accepted war as a bitter necessity forced upon it by the tragic stupidity of the circumstances. What happened was unwanted, and it came upon us with dramatic suddenness. The frightening crisis reached its crescendo almost overnight; yet its choking embrace was shattered with even greater switfness and with a thoroughness that was in no way foreseeable. The transformation was rapid, radical, and unenvisaged. The most precious prize of its long history was dopped into Israel's lap while it was hardly looking. As the rabbis of old would say, salvation came *b'heseach hada'as* while we were absentminded. "The help of God takes a wink of an eye." All the old sayings about messianic events took on a new and undreamed-of reality. Yet, all this might have been mere chance. But then came the realization that the utterly unexpected was the most expected, the event for which Jews had been longing through the ages, return to Zion and Jerusalem. That for which we had been least prepared was the most-longed-for.

To our surprise we discovered that if we were absentminded, we were not absent-hearted. Our hearts were wiser than our minds. Our hearts were expecting all the time and we did not know. It was not an expectation on the man-made level of history, waiting for political advantages and military victories. Such are the hopes of the mind, and the mind was caught unaware. The heart was expecting with messianic wisdom. Once again, we have to say it in the words of the teaching. "I sleep, but my heart waketh," commented the rabbis: "I have fallen asleep waiting for the end of my exile, but my heart is awake to redemption." [11] We have been awakened to a messianic hour in our history and found that our hearts were awake all the time. Thus we learned to understand that if we were absentminded, all the generations were watching us; if we thought to operate on a purely secular level, almost forgetful of the messianic vision, Jewish history had not changed its direction. We could not but recall that what we did not expect consciously was the expectation of the ages. And now it was happening before our own eyes, the vindication of our own hearts whose truth we so often denied.

What was not granted to any other generation was awarded to the people in Zion—an encounter with all Jewish history, a very real communion with all the generations. It was as if they were conversing with the patriarchs, walking with King David, listening to the voice of the prophets, comforting the martyrs. According to a midrashic legend, at the time of the revelation at Sinai, all the souls yet to be born in flesh were assembled with the contemporary generation to receive the Torah for all generations yet to come. When the present generation stood at the West Wall of the Temple in Zion again, all the generations whose eyes were longingly turned toward the event all through the ages, stood with them. The Wall recalled all "the walls" of the ghettos, of the dungeons, of the concentration camps, and testified that they were no mere oversight before God; it gave the Jew the assurance that somehow and somewhere in the world regimen there was an account from which will issue redemption to all the oppressed and persecuted generations. How? It was not important to be able to spell it out in detail. The decisive aspect of the experience was that "the people that walked in darkness have seen a great light." [12] It was for the entire people that ever walked in darkness that the light was received. As there was unity between the past and present, unity between the generations, so was there also a sense of unity, never in living memory experienced before in the midst of the contemporary generation. In those days of destiny we indeed were one people. Nowhere was the unifying power of the moment stronger than in the state of Israel itself. We are not thinking of the unity which is natural at moments of national peril, nor the unity of exaltation in the celebration of victory—there were no official, national, victory celebrations in Israel. We have in mind the unity of the spirit, forged in the awe and trembling of the messianic experience. The sensing of the messianic came to redeeming manifestation in the unity of all Israel. All Israel stood face to face with its universal destiny and came out of the experience with a new self-understanding. Perchance, this new self-understanding may not reach deep with many, it may not endure long with them. Yet, on it will be built the future of all Israel, because only what will be built on it has a future.

4

Is this the Messiah already? It is enough to look out of the window to realize that nothing could be further removed from the truth (unless he, too, came unexpectedly "like a thief"). But it is a messianic moment, in which the unexpected fruits of human endeavor reveal themselves as the mysterious manifestation of divine guidance of whose coming the heart was forever sure. Ever since the holocaust we have known that the great historic Jewries that perished will never be rebuilt again. We have known all these years that there is no way back to the past. But in which direction were we moving? Our steps were uncertain; reassurance was lacking; self-understanding was confused. But now we have seen a smile on the face of God. It is enough. It will be enough for a long time. We have been called to a new beginning. In the past, after every *hurban*, we built anew something new and different. After every destruction we were led to new enfoldings in the history of Judaism. After the first destruction, we created the synagogue, which represented a new phase of Judaism. After the second destruction, we created the Judaism of the Talmud. In our generation we experienced another *hurban*, the third destruction, the destruction of *Galut* Judaism, the liquidation of the Exile. Having found our way back to Zion in a messianic moment, we know that God is doing "a new thing; Now shall it spring forth," [13] the new in which—as in the past—the old will find home. What the nature of this "new thing" is going to be no one is able to discern at this early juncture; but we are able to define the theological significance of the circumstances in which it will have to grow and develop. Judaism in exile was lacking the wholeness of the existential reality within which the deed of practical faith could flourish. In the long history of the *Galut* the field of application was shrinking continually. In Babylon for instance, there were large areas closely settled by Jews who were permitted to live under their own laws and were internally ruled by their own Princes, whose authority over the Jews was recognized by the state. During the dark and Middle Ages there were many countries in which Jews enjoyed a high measure of internal autonomy, though the base of Judaic application to real issues of the human condition had been greatly narrowed. This narrowing of the base for the faith-applied deed narrowed further, although it was still available to some extent in the ghettos of modern times. The less intense the Jewish involvement in the majority culture and economy, the greater the chance for the authentically Jewish deed of daily existence. As the walls of the ghettos fell, Judaism was, more and more, reduced to the status of a mere religion. With the destruction of the great Jewries the basis for Judaic realization in historical reality has practically disappeared. Neither is it to be found in the communist world, where the only historical reality permitted to the Jew is one that divests him of his Judaic identity. On the other hand, in the democratic countries, where complete freedom of conscience is the rule, the very extent of freedom is the source of the problem. The involvement of the Jew in all the areas of human endeavor is an engagement in a world to which the comprehensive deed of Judaism cannot be applied. Judaism has never been as orphaned of living reality as in our days. Even among the pious, Judaism can only be a matter of private concern. Lacking the partnership of history, it is found to stagnate and to wither. However, at this moment of its greatest impoverishment of reality, destiny has blessed it with the opportunity for its fullest application to reality in the land of the fathers, in Zion and Jerusalem. For the first time, after nineteen centuries of a continually shrinking base of applicability, the challenge of a comprehensive human condition that requires the Judaic deed has been granted to the Jew. Today outside the Land of Israel the challenges to Judaism arise mainly from the Jew's involvement in a culture and society that is non-Jewish. Those problems are insoluble. Judaism was never meant to be realized in the midst of a Christian or Marxist civilization. One may fight delaying actions: if the diaspora were left to itself, the future of a significant form of Judaism would indeed be dim. This "new thing" that God is preparing in Zion, we do not know yet. But the unsolved problems, the numerous challenges, are addressed to Judaism from the foundation of a new comprehensive reality that asks for Judaism. Therein lies the promise of the future for all Jews. Will Jews understand it?

Examining the world scene, a Jew can see nowhere the presence of God in the history of the nations or religions—unless it be in the history of Israel and only through it also in the history of man. Eliminate Israel from history and there is no need for any reference to God. Without Israel everything is explainable and "expected." Economics, power politics, and psychology will explain all. Without Israel, man is self-explanatory. Only the reality of Israel resists explanation on the level of man-made history alone. Because of Israel the Jew knows that history is messianism, that God's guidance—however impenetrably wrapt in mystery—is never absent from the life of the nations.

VII. EPILOGUE

The holocaust having passed, the Jewish people were granted new hope through the realization of their age-old faith in the return to their ancient homeland. For nineteen centuries they were refugees among the nations. All through their *Galut* they kept faith with the land. Through their daily prayers for return and their uninterrupted mourning for Zion and Jerusalem they also gave notice that they never surrendered their claim to the land of their fathers. Whoever held sway over Eretz Yisrael was doing it under the continuous protest of the Jewish people. That protest may count for little in the power history of the nations—a protest of helplessness that could never be enforced. Yet the nations themselves underwrote it through the centuries of Israel's exile, without realizing it. Every time Jews were persecuted, whenever they were subjected to discrimination, treated like second-rate citizens and worse, their claim to their ancient homeland was validated by the world. The treatment they received from the nations meant: You are not one of us; you do not belong here. Go home! There has not been any essential difference in their plight whether in Christian and Moslem societies. It is true, the Moslems have been far less inhumane in their treatment of the Jews than the Christians. But even in Moslem countries there were persecutions and massacres, forcible conversions and plunder. In the best of circumstances, Jews were second-class citizens, living in precarious conditions, depending mostly on the good will of the ruler. To this day there are Moslem countries in the Near East where the law requires that Jewish children orphaned of their father must be taken from their families and brought up as Moslems. If the law is not much applied, it is mainly because since the establishment of the state of Israel most of the affected Jewish communities, after long centuries of domicile, left those countries. To the extent to which exile has been imposed upon the Jew by the powers that be, his claim to return to Eretz Yisrael has been conceded by implication even within the framework of power history. Of course, power history will not recognize such arguments. That is why it is power history. Its ultimate logic is, indeed, the gas chamber. Nevertheless, the claim is valid. The truth value of a protest like that of the Jewish people cannot be crushed by physical might. There are times even in power history, when a new spirit seems to descend upon the nations, heralding in a new and a better era, when a claim like that of the Jews is recognized. As a result, in 1920 the League

of Nations acknowledged the right of the Jewish people to a state
of their own within the historic boundaries of ancient Israel, a state
which in 1948, in a much reduced area, came into being with the
sanction of the international authority of the United Nations.

However, as long as the world still hangs on to the belief in the
viability of power history, such moments of a new spirit are short-
lived. It is because of this that the Jewish people find themselves today once again in a situation no less serious than the one which directly preceeded the holocaust in Europe. The climate of international
morals is very similar. One could see it during the tense weeks
immediately prior to the outbreak of the Six Day War. Dark
clouds were closing in on the little state of Israel. The Arab nations
were forging an iron ring of hatred, fortified by vast tank divisions
and air forces, around it. They vowed to erase the state from the
face of the earth in a holy war and to push the Israelis into the
sea, thus to make true an earlier vow of the ruler of Egypt that
the world was going to witness a massacre the likes of which it had
not known since the days of Genghis Khan. The world was ready
to witness. Once again there was impartiality as in the days of the
holocaust. Governments and churches, political and religious leaders, were prepared to commit once again the crime of genocide by
silence. The conscience of the world was as little in evidence as
in the time of the death camps and the crematoria. The United
Nations, lacking both a moral purpose and political effectiveness,
had become a farce on the international scene.

If the Arabs did not succeed with their plans, it was not because
of any discouragement on the part of the world's conscience. On
the contrary, the story of Israel's struggle for survival since the
Six Day War has shown that as no world conscience existed during
the holocaust, neither is it anything to be reckoned with these days.
In its various statements and resolutions on Israel, the Security
Council has been degraded to an anti-Israeli propaganda instrument of the Russo-Arab front. The Arabs can do no wrong, the
Israelis can do no right. As a result, the moral dignity and influence of the U.N. has been eroded. The U.N. is becoming more and
more the image of the defunct League of Nations prior to its
extinction. Since the Six Day War we have witnessed the French
betrayal of Israel under the hypocritical guise of furthering the

cause of peace. International indifference toward the plight of
Israel has also been spreading. As far as the Jewish people are
concerned, the place of the Nazis has been taken over by Soviet
Russia. If not genocide, ethnocide is being committed, and its
victims are the three million Jews of the Soviet Republic. A policy
is being ruthlessly pursued that aims at destroying every vestige
of Jewish identity. The official propaganda against Judaism as well
as against the state of Israel is as unbridled and abusive as that of
the worst of its kind in Nazi Germany. All this is done under the
pretense of attacking that international monster, Zionism, which is
described in the language of the Protocol of the Elders of Zion forgery. The guise may be anti-Zionism; the language and the contents
are in the style of the most virulent kind of antisemitism known in
history.

As in the days of Hitler, this kind of calculated venomous propaganda finds much understanding in the world today. It can be
disseminated in the name of progress and concern for freedom for
the oppressed. It is accepted by many, even though it is carried
on by the most determined and most dangerous imperialistic power
in modern times. It is not ridiculous that Israel should be called the
aggressor and accused of expansionist colonialism and imperialism
by Soviet Russia? The Soviet colossus is the power that concluded
the infamous pact with Nazi Germany and thus eased the Nazi's
way to the outbreak of the Second World War. The Soviet Union
attacked Finland and incorporated part of its territory. During the
Second World War it absorbed vast territories of neighboring
countries, and swallowed up the Baltic states. Later, it crushed
the hopes for freedom in Hungary and Czechoslovakia, And this
conquering empire is not laughed out of international discourse
when it condemns Israel in Nazi language as an aggressor and
oppressor. Does anyone believe that Russia has been pouring
weapons into Egypt at the cost of billions of dollars out of pity
for the poor Arabs? It is strange how blind the world becomes as
soon as the apparent thrust of a conquering power is directed
against the Jews. What we are witnessing is an exercize in power
politics of the first magnitude. How blind are the Arabs who, because of their irrational hatred of the state of Israel, are willing to
opt for a future under the Russian yoke rather than to live in

peace and mutual respect with Israel! Experience has shown that once the Russians gain a foothold anywhere, they do not surrender it unless compelled to do so. Who is to compel them to surrender their grip over the Middle East and the Mediterranean once they are firmly established there? The world, because of its insensitivity to Jewish survival, is moving into a nuclear confrontation between the super-powers. The earth itself will become one global crematorium.

Once again the churches have adopted their historic attitude toward the Jew. Of course, they are not antisemitic; they are only anti-Zionist, accepting the Russian definition of Zionism. Anti-Zionism has become the purified version of old-fashioned antisemitism and anti-Judaism. Once again, the Vatican is as "impartial" as ever. When Arab guerillas murder innocent civilians, even outside Israel, set bombs in airplanes, business offices in foreign lands, knowingly ambush and massacre children, the Vatican observes "a delicate reserve." But when Israel retaliates by destroying planes in an Arab land, first making sure—at risk to the lives of its own soldiers—that no one should get hurt, a cable of sympathy from the Vatican is in order. Some of the churches started once again preaching to the Jews about human values. They who were silent when Hitler's armies were conquering Europe, have suddenly awakened to their responsibility and demand that Israel surrender all conquered territories, without any regard to its future safety and survival. Our generation has seen the tragedy of millions of refugees wandering all over the globe. Refugees from Greece to Turkey, from Turkey to Greece; from India to Pakistan, from Pakistan to India; refugees in Germany from Poland and Czechoslovakia—tens of millions of them. The problem has been partly solved through resettlement, partly it has remained unsolved to this day. The world conscience, on the religious as well as secular level, remained unruffled. Only in the case of the Palestinian refugees has a Christian conscience come to sudden life. This is the only case of professional political refugees in the world. In a saner atmosphere, the problem could have been solved through compensation and resettlement, on the basis of a population exchange; the little state of Israel absorbed more than a million Jews from Arab countries who were forced to leave all their possessions behind them. Of the Palestinian refugees Nasser said that "if they return to Israel, Israel will cease to exist." Who are these people who dare talk to Jews about humane treatment of refugees? The same that showed a murderous indifference toward the plight of millions of Jews as they were driven in cattle trucks all across Europe; the same people who witnessed the slaughter of one and a half million Jewish children without moving a finger to help, often preventing the implementation of any plans of assistance. Now they are eager to solve the Arab refugee problem at the cost of the destruction of the state of Israel and the slaughter of its citizens. If at all possible, the world conscience is sicker today than it was during the Nazi era, because it is more hypocritical.

2

Essentially, this is still the holocaust world. What happened then, may happen again, anywhere and everywhere. It is no less conceivable today than it was in the twenties in Germany. On the contrary! In the meantime mankind has become even more desensitized to the spectacle of inhumanity and barbarism. The disintegration of value standards has been proceeding apace. The Jewish response must be the one given by the Jews of Israel in the Six Day War: Never again! If it is to die, it is better to die with a gun in one's hand than in a concentration camp or gas chamber. Resist! Resist! Resist! It must be incorporated in the very core of Jewish education until it produces an instinctive reaction of resistance to any attack. However, an attitude of this kind must not be developed on the basis of desperation or with a sense of hopelessness. In this way it would destroy the historic identity of the Jew. "Never again!" must have an ethical motivation and it must be supported by an understanding of the historic role of Judaism and of the Jewish people and its conscious acceptance.

One is morally obligated to resist evil not only if it attacks others, but even if it attacks onself. Anyone who denies to any man the right to life, to self-realization, to equality and freedom denies humanity. It is my obligation to humanity to defend myself. Since every victory of evil emboldens it to greater depredations, it is one's duty to resist it at every point. It is especially so in the case of the Jew. Antisemitism has been the most deeply rooted and most continuous propensity of Western civilization. It could, therefore, always most easily be activated for the demoralization of any society. For this reason the cause of the Jew in the world or as we may also say, the cause of faith history, in a sense contains all the causes. A world immune to antisemitism will be a world of moral integrity. To fight for Jewish survival is being in the forefront of man's struggle for human dignity, freedom, and peace.

However, our strength can only come from an understanding of our role in history and our willingness to accept it. The Jewish people and, together with them the state of Israel, are isolated in the world. Certainly among the mighty and powerful they have hardly any reliable friends. But if at this stage of human civilization it were otherwise, they would not be Jewish. If any of the great powers would pour as many airplanes, weapons, and as much manpower assistance into the state of Israel—half as much and half as generously—as Russia does in the case of Egypt, Israel would have entered power history. It would be a minor accessory to it. But Israel does not have the oil resources, the vast territories, the population masses, the strategic position to render it a factor in power history. That is why it is Israel. As a state, Israel is in exile in power history just as Jews as a scattered people were in exile in "the wilderness of the nations."[1] Israel's strength must come from the same resources from which the survival power of the Jew came in the past—from within the Jewish people, from the spirit within the Jew, from his heart and mind. The relative isolation of the state of Israel in the international game of power politics is a natural phenomenom. Even though little Israel has been surprisingly effective in war, what does it amount to in the present-day power constellation? Even as a state, Israel lives in faith history. Such is the spirit of its people.

A few years before the outbreak of the Six Day War I visited one of the northernmost kibbutzim. Looking out of the window I was looking into Syria; the frontier was in the backyard. In our discussion with some of the *vatikim* (the elders), I asked them on what they were relying, living so close to continuous danger to their lives and the lives of their children. Since the kibbutz was prominent in the atheistic leftist Kibbutz movement, I broadened

the question and asked them how they could imagine that the
handful of Israeli Jews could make a stand against the tens of
millions of Arabs that surround them on all sides. Did they believe
in some kind of a master-race theory that would enable little Israel
to be victorious against the alliance of the entire Arab world? Their
answer came to me as a surprise, and was characteristic: We believe
in human progress. We rely on it. The meaning was clear; they
staked their very existence on their belief that ultimately it will be
possible to reach an understanding with their Arab neighbors and
to live in peace with them. I realized then that the state of Israel,
even among secularist Jews, existed in faith history. There has
never been a less militaristic army than that of Israel. There has
never been a victorious army as desirous of peace as the Israelis.
Israel went to war as a bitter necessity. Everyone going away
quietly from his shop, from his school, his field, his job, his kibbutz.
There was no "patriotic" send-off, no flower bouquets and kisses
thrown at the departing soldiers by beautiful girls. No public
farewell scenes. Israel went to war silently. And came back in
silence, without hurrahs and victory parades. There has never
been a people struggling as earnestly against being brutalized itself
by the necessities of continuous warfare as Israel. Anyone who
desires to know the truth can easily ascertain the unexampled
humanitarian treatment of the Arab population in the conquered
territories. Every possible effort is being made to control internal
sabotage and terrorism. However, the average Arab in the occupied
territories enjoys more civic freedom, more freedom of the press,
more freedom of peaceful assembly, more freedom to criticize
Israel in speech and print than even the average Russian enjoys
in Russia, certainly more than the citizens of the Baltic states
enjoy in their homeland, much more than the Czechs and Slovaks
have in Czechoslovakia or the Hungarians in Hungary. Israel does
not live in power history; but it does live in the same time-space
continuum in which power history is being enacted. It is a form
of Jewish tragedy that in order to maintain itself Israel has to use
instruments of power history. It is its glory that it is striving con-
scientiously and with considerable success to do it by applying
the spirit and the methods of faith history.

3

Numerous perils are besetting the very existence of the state of Israel. Might it not one day fall victim to an unfavorable international power constellation? The question is justified, but not more so than the question as to whether the power colossi themselves will survive.

The plight of those who, like the Jews, live mainly in faith history is the moral barometer of the world. So was it in the past, so is it today. For this reason the peril that threatens the Jew is a warning to mankind. The danger that threatens Jewish existence is the measure of the moral crisis of the world. It is history's danger signal. Conditions of the collapse of human values facilitate the depredation of power history. The warning was not heeded at the ascent of nazism to power in Germany. The result was the Second World War. The warning is scarcely being heeded now and the world is moving toward its encounter with the ultimate disaster, the thermonuclear conflagration. Power has never been as stupid as in our times. As the result of the dialectical self-defeat of power, power history is objectively at an end. For the great powers to pursue a course as if this were still the era of power history is to doom the world to face ultimate catastrophe and nothingness. Power history is at an end; man must change course or perish. The balance of terror by which the world continues to exist today will not save it for long. Man cannot live by terror alone. One day the delicate balance is bound to break down. The only hope for man would be to bring power history consciously to a close. Will he be able to do it? It is more than doubtful.

The era of the holocaust was history's great challenge to affirm and to defend fundamental human values. Man has failed tragically. The years after the holocaust, because of the monstrous increase in human power, should have brought about the spiritual transformation of the age. It did not happen. A much more dangerous man lives on with a soul infected by the holocaust betrayal. What of tomorrow? The anxiety, the despair, the nihilism, so widely spread all over the globe, indicate that many, especially among the young, do not believe in the saving transformation of mankind.

International cynicism might bring about the downfall of a power politically as insignificant a state as Israel. But when international cynicism sinks to such a level the future of man will be no less questionable than that of the state of Israel. As in the past the Jew in exile was the crystallization point for the moral direction history was taking, so today the destiny of the Jewish people in Zion is that same point of crystallization. Only that today it ought to be obvious to all that in the direction of power and political cynicism lies the road to ultimate disaster for all. The peril is the peril of all; and whatever slight hope there remains must be hope for all.

4

How much hope is there? Looking at this holocaust world of ours one beholds very little that may give one much encouragement. We do not even know whether the next generation of man will have enough life-sustaining air to breathe. The problem of external pollution in the widest sense of the word, of foul air, of poisoned rivers and lakes, of atomic weaponry, of filthy ghettos, cannot be solved without the prior solution of the problem of internal pollution, the pollution of the minds and hearts of men who insist on living on in an anachronistic power history. For that, however, there is but little hope. No one knows it better than the Jew, judging this civilization by what he received at its hands. Yet, no one is entitled to more optimism than the Jew, who having lived in faith history has survived to the very end of power history. He believes in the viability of faith history. It is no more rational to believe in it today than it was when he first appeared on the scene of history. He has more reason to trust his enterprise today than he had when the call of God first reached the soul of his father Abraham. If there is no future for faith history, then the Jew has no past. For the Jew, his past is the guarantee of the future, not only his own but that of man. To the extent that the future of man is hopeless, Israel's future too is hopeless.

As a Jew, I can believe in the future of man only because I believe in the future of Israel. I believe in the future of man only because I believe that power history will make room for faith

history. I believe it because ever since the destruction of the second
Jewish state in the year 69 C.E., to the extent to which Israel has
survived, power history has made room for faith history. I believe
in that future because the Jewish endurance of nineteen centuries
of a violent civilization testifies to it; because the Jew who still
well remembers its beginnings, is also present at this its contemporary phase of its self-frustrating disintegration.

One might of course say: this is merely faith! But can anyone
entertain hope of today's man in the future without some faith?
The question is, in what does one place one's faith: in the man of
history or in the God of history? As a Jew, looking at man, I can
have no faith in his future. Yet, I do have faith in man's future.
Jewish history forbids me to have faith in man; Jewish history
bids me to have faith in the future of man.

I have faith in the future of man because of Abraham Seidman,[2]
the Jew in the Warsaw Ghetto, the kind of Jew whom Judaism
produced in every generation in tens of thousands, a pious, modest,
hardworking *pater familias* at the same time scholarly, not in a
professional sense, but simply because it was the duty of every
Jew to study and to know the Torah. He had been taken from the
Ghetto to the *Umschlagplatz* to be sent to Auschwitz. There was
still some time before the transport was to leave. How did Abraham Seidman spend the few remaining minutes? He wrote a letter
to his children taking leave of them forever and asking them for
forgiveness should he ever have offended or hurt them. Because
of what man did to Abraham Seidman I have no faith in man,
because of the Jew Seidman I have faith in the future of man.

I have faith in the future of man because of Itzik Rosenzweig.[3]
Itzik was a Jew somewhere in Slovakia, a Jew like A. Seidman in
Warsaw. He made a living by raising poultry. One day he and his
family were squeezed into the cattle cars, in which hundreds of
other Jews were pressed to suffocation. In the car there was despair
all around him; outside a celebrating population of former neighbors was jeering at him and deriding him. He begged them: Please,
go to my house and give water and food to the poultry. They had
nothing to eat or drink all day. This was just one of the thousands
of confrontations that in those days were happening between Judaism and Western civilization, between power history and faith

history. Because of what man did to Itzik Rosenzweig I have no faith in man; because of Itzik, in spite of it all, I have faith in the future of man.

Of tomorrow or the day after tomorrow we know nothing. How long the process of the final disintegration of this, by history already discarded, civilization will go on; when man will begin to enjoy the first fruits of another, new and better day, no one can know. But one thing we do know. If ever there was a time for the Jew to persevere, it is now. If ever it made sense for him to accept his role in history, it is at this hour of dusk and dawn. Never was he more truly a witness to God in history than at this juncture of history, when all this earth is in jeopardy.

NOTES

1. Quoted by Arthur D. Morse, *While Six Million Died, A Chronicle of American Apathy,* New York, Random House, 1967, p. 30.
2. Ibid., p. 291.
3. Ibid.
4. Ibid., pp. 85, 336.
5. Ibid., p. 335.
6. Ibid., p. 263.
7. Ibid., p. 95.
8. Ibid., p. 128.
9. Ibid., p. 95.
10. Ibid., pp. 128 and 250.
11. Ibid., quoted by Morse, p. 347.
12. Ibid., p. 259.
13. Guenter L. Lewy, *The Catholic Church and Nazi Germany.* New York, McGraw-Hill, 1964, p. 100.
14. Ibid., p. 106.
15. Ibid., p. 108.
16. Ibid., p. 112.
17. Morse, op. cit., p. 13.
18. Ibid., p. 14.
19. The opinion of Morse, p. 362.
20. The spelling of the name is transcribed from the Hebrew text of Weiss-mandel. It may not be correct; but those familiar with the local history of the time are sure to recognize it. To establish the exact spelling of the Cardinal's name would be a waste of time. It matters little.
21. *Min Hamezar,* 24.
22. Ibid., p. 25.
23. Toynbee, Arnold, J., *A Story of History,* Vol. IX, p. 433.
24. G. Lewy, op. cit., p. 274.
25. Edward H. Flannery, *The Anguish of the Jews,* New York: Macmillan, 1965.
26. See the magazine, *Continuum,* Autumn 1966.
27. Flannery, Op. cit., p. 276.
28. Ibid., p. 63.
29. Ibid., p. 72.
30. Ibid., p. 91.
31. Ibid., p. 72.
32. Ibid., p. 40.
33. Ibid., p. 96.

34. Quoted in *The Anguish of the Jews*, Notes, p. 312.
35. Ibid., pp. 45, 61.
36. Ibid., p. 23.
37. Ibid., 277.
38. *Talmud Babli, B'khorot,* 2b, and *Sanhedrin,* 63b.
39. Flannery, op. cit., 274.
40. See Chapter II, the section, *"Judaism in the Post-Christian Era."*
41. Quoted by John Cogley in The *Sunday Times,* June 13, 1965.
42. Cf. the article by H. Trevor Roper in *Commentary* magazine.
43. K. Shabbetai, *As Sheep to the Slaughter? The Myth of Cowardice.* with a Foreword by Gideon Hausner, New York and Tel Aviv: World Federation of the Bergen-Belsen Survivors Associations, 1963.
44. Hannah Arendt, *Eichman in Jerusalem,* New York, The Viking Press, 1964 paperback edition, pp. 11–12.
45. Op. cit., p. 54.
46. See, for instance, the material assembled in *Kiddush Hashem,* edited by S. Niger, N. Y., in Yiddish.
47. Cf., *Sefer Milhamot Ha'Gettaot,* eds. Zuckerman and Basok, (Tel Aviv: Ha'Kibutz Ha' M'uhad, 1954).
48. Ibid., p. 557.
49. *Kiddush Hashem,* op. cit., p. 365.
50. *Sefer Milhamot Ha'Gettaot,* op. cit., p. 557.
51. *Notes from the Warsaw Ghetto,* New York, Toronto and London. McGraw Hill, 1958, pp. 273–274.
52. *As Sheep to the Slaughter,* op. cit., pp. 45–46.
53. *Notes from the Warsaw Ghetto,* op. cit., p. 322; *Kiddush Hashem,* op. cit., p. 125.
54. *The Root and the Bough,* ed. Leo W. Schwartz, New York, Rinehart, 1949; the opening sentences in the chapter, *Apologia of a Physician.*
55. Cf. *The Informed Heart,* by Bruno Bettelheim, New York, The Free Press of Glencoe, 1964.

NOTES TO CHAPTER II

1. Malcohm Hay, *The Food of Pride,* Boston, The Beacon Press, 1950, p. 22.
2. *Midrash Rabba, Kohelet,* 3, 19.
3. Quoted by Thomas, J. J. Altizer in his, *Mircea Eliade and the Dialectic of the Sacred,* Philadelphia: The Westminister Press, 1963, p. 27.
4. Altizer, *Radical Theology and the Death of God,* New York: The Bobbs-Merrill Co. 1966, p. 99.
5. Harvey Cox, *The Secular City,* New York: Macmillan Paperbacks 1966, pp. 71–72.
6. *Mircea Eliade,* p. 26.
7. W. Hamilton, and Altizer, *Radical Theology,* p. 36.
8. Hamilton, op. cit., p. 165; Altizer, op. cit., p. 182; also *Mircea Eliade,* p. 18.
9. Cox, op. cit., p. 72.

10. G. Vahanian, *The Death of God*, New York: George Braziller, pp. 8, 175, 181–183.
11. Altizer, *Radical Theology*, pp. 103–109.
12. Vahanian op. cit., p. 46.
13. Quoted by Vahanian, ibid., p. 46.
14. *Mircea Eliade* op. cit., p. 65.
15. See P.M., Van Buren, *The Secular Meaning of the Gospel*, New York: The Macmillan Co., 1963, p. 11; cf. also R. Bultman's essay, *History of Salvation and History* in his *Existence and Faith*, New York: Living Age Books, 1960.
16. *Radical Theology*, p. 110.
17. *Mircea Eliade*, p. 33.
18. We add this qualification in order to avoid the need for a discussion of the idea of the holy as a divine attribute.
19. *Mircea Eliade*, p. 18; *Radical Theology*, p. 128.
20. Hamilton, op. cit., p. 18.
21. *Radical Theology*, p. 187.
22. Ibid., p. 126.
23. Cf., for instance, *Ibid.*, pp. 12, 95, 152, 185.
24. Cox does argue that "the biblical God's hiddenness stands at the very center of the doctrine of God"—op. cit., p. 258. He is right speaking of the Hebrew Bible; I cannot see how this may apply to the Savior God of the New Testament.
25. Dietrich Bonhoeffer, *Letters and Papers from Prison*, New York: Macmillan Paperbacks 1962, pp. 168, 205.
26. Cf. Cox's opening chapter, *"The Biblical Sources of Secularization* also pp. 19, 72–73; also Vahanian, pp. 61, 67–68.

NOTES TO CHAPTER III

1. Job 42: 5–6.
2. Ibid., 2: 9.
3. Albert Camus, *Resistance, Rebellion, and Death*, New York, A. Kriuff, 1961, p. 32.
4. Ibid., p. 28.
5. Leon Poliakov, *The Harvest of Hate*, Syracuse, Syracuse Univ. Press, 1954, p. 214.
6. Camus, *The Plague*, New York, A. Krioff, 1957, p. 231.
7. Camus, *Resistance, Rebellion and Death*, p. 71.
8. *The Root and the Bough, The Epic of an Enduring People*, op cit., p. 28.
9. Ibid., p. 40.
10. Ibid., p. 234.
11. Hillel Seidman, *Yoman Ghetto Varsha*. Tel Aviv, Uma Unoledet, 5706 A.M., p. 315.
12. See, for example, *Notes From the Warsaw Ghetto: The Journal of Emanuel Ringelblum*, op. cit., p. 330.
13. See Poliakov, op. cit.

14. Ibid., p. 157.
15. Ibid., p. 222.
16. I.e., One; the last word of the verse, Hear O Israel. . . .
17. *Talmud Babli, Berakhot,* 61 b.
18. Ringelblum, op. cit., pp. 83, 88.
19. Seidman, op. cit., p. 215.
20. *The Root and the Bough,* op. cit., p. 200.

NOTES TO CHAPTER IV

1. Isaiah 51: 17; Jeremiah, 16:7.
2. Isaiah 45: 6–7.
3. Cf. Saadia Gaon, *Emunoth VeDeoth;* Maimonides, *Moreh N'bukhim,* III.
4. Deuteronomy 30: 15–18.
5. Isaiah 13: 9, 11.
6. Jeremiah 12: 1.
7. Habakkuk 1: 13.
8. Job 11, 13–16.
9. Ibid., 42: 7.
10. Psalms 89: 9.
11. Exodus 15: 18.
12. Talmud Babli; *Gittin,* 56 b.
13. This is true, notwithstanding the attempt by some talmudic teachers to interpret the phenomenon as an appropriate balancing of justice between this world and the world to come. See, for instance, *Talmud Babli, Kiddushin,* 39 b. Medieval Jewish philosophers often follow the same inadequate argument.
14. Not to be confused with the Christian interpretation of Jewish history, mentioned earlier in the text. The Jew says: Because of our sins. The Christian maintains: Because of your sins. The one is critical self-judgment; the other, hypocritical judging of others.
15. Ezekiel 8: 12.
16. Malachi 3: 13–15.
17. Talmud Babli, *Kiddushin,* 39 b.
18. According to Rabbenu Yona, quoted in *Kesef Mishne,* Maimonides, *Hilkhot Tefilla,* 2, 2.
19. Psalms 44: 24–27.
20. Ibid., 13: 2.
21. Ibid., 10: 12.
22. Isaiah 49: 14.
23. *Bereshit Rabba,* 29, 14.
24. Jeremiah 11: 20.
25. Habakkuk 1: 12.
26. Job 13: 15.
27. Psalms 145: 18.
28. Ibid., 145: 9.

29. Ibid., 31: 24.
30. *Midrash T'hillim,* 31.
31. Isaiah 45: 15.
32. Ibid., 8, 17.
33. Ecclesiastes 7: 14. More in keeping with the Hebrew original, and in conformity with the manner in which the verse was understood by the rabbis in the Talmud, we depart somewhat from the rendering of the verse in the R. V.
34. *Talmud Babli. Hagiga,* 15 a.
35. See our discussion of the quotation from Isaiah and the concept of creation connected with it in our book, *God, Man and History,* ch. 9.
36. Ezekiel 33: 11.
37. Deuteronomy, 10, 17.
38. *Talmud Babli.* Yoma, 69 a. For the references to Jeremiah, Daniel, Ezra, cf. *Jeremiah,* 32, 18; *Daniel,* 9, 4; *Nehemiah,* 9, 32.

NOTES TO CHAPTER V

 1. Isaiah 43: 12.
 2. Sifrei,
 3. Deuteronomy 7: 7.
 4. Isaiah 43: 10.
 5. Cf. Rashi's commentary on Genesis 1: 1.
 6. Amos 3: 2.
 7. Quoted from *Galut* by Yitzhak F. Baer, New York: Schocken Library, 12, 1947, p. 26.
 8. Genesis 12: 1.
 9. Ibid., 15: 13.
10. Cf. f. i., *Talmud Babli, B'rakhot,* 59 a.
11. Genesis 15: 13.
12. Cf., Isaiah 66: 1.
13. This is a quote from André Schwarz-Bart's, *The Last of the Just.* The next episode is described in a letter by the father of the child, published in *Kiddush Hashem,* ed. S. Niger, N. Y., 5707 A.M. The last episode referred to is recorded in *Notes from the Warsaw Ghetto,* the Journal of Emanuel Ringelblum.
14. Cf. Isaiah, 63: 9.
15. *Shaar Ha'gmul* in *Hiddushei Ha'Ramban,* Part I., p. 193, ed. B'nei Brak, 5719 A.M.
16. We are not unaware of the biblical verse that asserts that "all His ways are justice." (Deut. 32: 4) Obviously, the midrashic statement we have quoted in our text about the creation of the world by mercy and justice is not in keeping with such a reading. However, the Hebrew Bible does not have: "all His ways are justice." But, "all His ways are *Mishpat.*" I have shown in a recent work how misleading it is to translate the biblical *Mishpat* as "justice" in the sense of Western civilization. See the chapter, "The Biblical Meaning of Justice," in my *Man and God, Studies in Biblical Theology,* Detroit: Wayne State University Press, 1969.

17. *Talmud Babli, Sanhedrin,* 39 b.
18. Ibid., 89 b.
19. Nicholas Berdyaev, *The Meaning of History,* Cleveland, World Publishing Co., 1962.
20. *Talmud Babli, Yoma,* 69 b.

NOTES TO CHAPTER VI

1. Isaiah 2: 3–4.
2. Ibid., 19: 25.
3. *Talmud Babli, K'tubot,* 110 b.
4. Saadia, *Emmunot V'Deoth,* 3, 7; cf. also Maimonides, *Moreh N'Bukhim,* 2, 29.
5. Isaiah 43: 21; 44: 2, 21.
6. Habakkuk 2: 4.
7. *Talmud Babli, Kiddushin,* 40 b.
8. Deuteronomy 3: 25.
9. *Talmud Babli, Sota,* 14 a.
10. Psalms, 118: 23.
11. *Midrash Rabba* on the Song of Songs, 5: 2.
12. Isaiah, 9: 1.
13. Ibid., 43: 19.

NOTES TO EPILOGUE

1. Ezekiel, 20: 35.
2. For this episode see *Yoman Warsaw,* the Warsaw Ghetto diary of his son, Hillel, op. cit.
3. M. D. Weissmandel, op. cit. 32.

INDEX